CATHERINE TEKAKWITHA

Catherine Tegahkouita Iroquoise
morte en Odeur de Sainteté dans le Canada

This picture is a photograph of an engraving in the German edition,
dated 1742, of the *Lettres Edifiantes,* which was derived from the
original painting of Catherine made in 1681, from memory, by
Claude Chauchetière, S. J.

CATHERINE TEKAKWITHA

BY

DANIEL SARGENT

LONGMANS, GREEN AND CO.

NEW YORK · TORONTO

1936

SARGENT
CATHERINE TEKAKWITHA

COPYRIGHT · 1936
BY DAÑIEL SARGENT

FIRST EDITION

To

FATHER LEONARD FEENEY, S.J.

CONTENTS

CHAPTER I

A RETICENT LETTER

On the fourteenth of October 1682, a Frenchman living in Canada began a letter to a Frenchman living in France. He had seen many wonders in Canada, and was therefore eager to tell about them. At the same time he was well aware that only half what a man away from home writes home has any chance of being believed. He would almost surely, if he wrote with enthusiasm, be accused of exaggeration. Therefore he chose to write as laconically as possible, and to understate everything. If he wrote about marvels as if they were not marvels he might possibly be believed.

In front of him spread the St. Lawrence River. Looking north over it he could see the shore where now stands the city of Montreal. The river was such a river as nobody had ever dreamed of in France : it was not a river, it was an inundation. He tried to write about its immensity as if it excited in him no wonderment. He did not entirely succeed, but he did his best and his account of it is not insober.

"The place where we are is so high that the waters of this great river fall here with a loud roar, and roll over many cascades, which frighten one to look at. The water foams as you see it do under a mill-wheel. We nevertheless readily pass over it every day in our bark canoes. And I cannot help saying that one must be crazy to run the rapids, as we do, without fear of being drowned!" *

It can be seen from this that the writer had imagination enough to be thrilled by the St. Lawrence River. Yet there were other marvels in Canada which thrilled him even more. He was a missionary, a priest, a Jesuit, a certain Father Chauchetière, born in Poitiers in 1645, who was now only thirty-seven years old, and who had spent seven years already among the Indians of Canada whom he was trying to Christianize. The great astonishment of his life as a missionary had not been the size of the St. Lawrence River (he had heard of that in France), but the piety which he had found among the Indians at his St. Lawrence Mission. He had expected to be horrified by the Indians even though he was willing to give his life for them. Instead he had been edified by them. But how was he going to convince the Jesuit Superior, to whom he was writing his letter, of this Indian holiness? He began impersonally, cautiously, statistically: "We have a chapel 25 feet wide, and nearly 60 feet long. We have three bells — and the savages will soon have another bell, weighing 200 livres, to complete the harmony. — There are sixty cabins — that is to say, from 120 to 150 families, as there are at least two in each cabin."

Then he described a thing harder to have believed: the fervor of the Indians. Lest it be thought that he believed that

* The entire letter can be found on pp. 167-89, vol. LXII. of the magnificent seventy-three volumes edited by R. G. Thwaites, *The Jesuit Relations and Allied Documents,* published in Cleveland, 1896-1901; a collection which forms a background to this book, and which is hereafter referred to in the notes as Thwaites.

such fervor existed simply because he wanted it to exist, he dwelt on the inconvenience of this fervor : it led the Indians to adopt immoderate penances, and forced him to step in and restrain them. Only grudgingly did he add, as the sole flash of his enthusiasm, that "they would be admired in France if what they do were known there."

Finally he came to what was most incredible of all :

"During the past two years their fervor has greatly increased since God has removed from this world one of these devout savage women who live like nuns, and she died with the reputation of sanctity. We cease not to say Masses to thank God for the graces that we believe we receive every day through her intercession. Journeys are continually made to her tomb ; and the savages, following her example, have become better Christians than they were. We daily see wonders worked through her intercession. Her name was Catherine Tekak-witha."

If we read these words twice, we see that they mean definitely that Father Chauchetière thought he had seen a saint : a real saint, an Indian saint, among the savages on the St. Lawrence River. He did not tell his own impressions of her. He did not divulge that he believed she had appeared to him twice in heaven-sent apparitions since her death, and that she had prophesied to him things that to his mind came true. What he recounted was common knowledge. Let his Superior make of it what he could.

The reticence with which Chauchetière chose to speak was, no doubt, wise. In telling of extraordinary things it is well to speak calmly and objectively if one wishes to be believed.

But the question arises : why did Father Chauchetière consider the sanctity of this Indian girl so little to be expected, so incredible even ? Why did he think that he had to appear so very, very calm, in order to be believed ? After all, he was a Christian priest writing to another Christian priest, and he could assume as a matter of course that miracles were believed in, and that it was considered as past contradiction that God was literally every day in France bringing to pass conversions no less startling than that of St. Paul, when as at a flash of lightning he had completely reversed the course of his life.

The answer, I think, is not difficult to find. Father Chauchetière and the European Christians of his day believed that God could be expected to make saints out of Europeans, for he had something to make them out of. Savages on the other hand were held scarcely to exist. They had only begun life. They were children. They seemed to lack any kind of a past because they had no European past, and they resembled in their nakedness and love of trinkets those Europeans who had least past : new-born babes. When the first European explorers saw the American Indians they called them savages not to insinuate that they were animals, or necessarily cruel, not indeed to insult them, but rather to pity them. They had been living outside of life. Grown of body, they were infants. They had no history.

Yet, really, Tekakwitha's ancestors were an old people. Not merely that they had had as many ancestors as any other man alive, but they remembered those ancestors. They carried the past with them in their traditions, from generation to generation. Their poverty did not necessarily mean they had always been poor. Much less did it mean that they had not played a dramatic rôle in human history. Primitive or near-primitive we may call them, but what gives drama to life — that is religion — exists often more sublimely among the primitives than among those with a little bit higher culture.* The ancestors of Catherine had been suffering and longing for ages. They had not waited, like care-free animals — as the romantics would have it — until with the coming of the Christians they acquired such concepts as eternal salvation to bother their heads with. The gaining of salvation had been their age-long preoccupation and occupation. Their campaign through the centuries had been to circumvent evil and death. They had made good marches and false marches, but they had always marched ; they had always been growing older and older with marching, always more weighed down with their accumulating past experience.

Behind Tekakwitha lay the past of Tekakwitha's ancestors, but also behind her in another sense lay some European past : the effort of Christian Europe in the sixteenth and seventeenth centuries to give its Faith to the new worlds which had lately been discovered.

Catherine Tekakwitha's life is indirectly a part of European history, and most especially of French history. She would never have been when and where she was in holiness without the great resurgence of Christian ardor in France during the

---

* For a complete discussion of the controversies concerning the origin of religion, and for a sane conclusion, see W. Schmidt, *The Origin and Growth of Religion*, translated by H. J. Rose, New York, 1931, or the larger work of which this is a summary, *Ursprung der Gottesidee*, 5 vols.

first half of the seventeenth century. The opportunity for spiritual ascent was prepared for her by very heroic missionary endeavors which, though they were not of age-long duration, had an epic quality, such as only Father Chauchetière can be excused from not recognizing, for he was himself but a part of that epic.

If we look at the past of Catherine's ancestors, as Father Chauchetière did not and could not (for the delvers into it had not yet performed their task), and if we look at the story of the French missionaries, then the spiritual blossoming of this Catherine becomes a climax of a long drama. Instead of exclaiming as Chauchetière did, "How suddenly she has come," our sigh is, "How long, how long, the world waited!"

CHAPTER II

THE ALGONQUIANS

CATHERINE's mother can be called both an Algonquin and an Algonquian. She can be called an Algonquin because it is the name which the French gave to her mother's tribe in the seventeenth century when they found it a hundred miles up the St. Lawrence River from Quebec, and wished to call the tribe as near as they could to what it called itself. She can be called an Algonquian, because that is the name which the Smithsonian Institute of Washington, D. C., gave gratuitously in the nineteenth century to all the tribes in America which spoke a language perceptibly related to that of the Algonquins. What does it mean to be an Algonquin? Or lest we grow too local, what does it mean to be an Algonquian?

If we look at a map whereon all those lands occupied by the Algonquians at the time of the coming of the White Men were marked red, we might think it was a very imperial thing to be an Algonquian. The Algonquians owned, by right of hunting in them, a half of all of habitable British North America south of the Esquimaux, and all of what is now the rich industrial and commercial sea-board of the United States from Canada to Carolina, and the greater part of the Mississippi valley, and the whole of the northern frontier of the United States, and scattered parts of the Rocky Mountains, and a few valleys in California. The Algonquians were the most numerous of American Indians north of the Rio Grande, and the most wide-spread. And the lands they occupied are not only now good lands to build on ; they were then good lands to hunt in.

But the Algonquians did not really have an empire. They not only had no political unity, but they had no unity at all that they themselves recognized. They had no idea that the scientists would class them together, and had not even any name for themselves. They were simply wandering tribes, some of which knew they were related by blood to those nearest them. They were less than wandering tribes, they were wandering groups, families with a rudimentary patriarchal government. Their empire had no roads, no bounds. The animals they hunted were in a sense their patrimony, but not the soil on which those animals trod. They considered the earth as general as we consider the air. They had no pride in an Algonquian Empire, which did not exist, and no pride in the name Algonquian which they had not coined.

At first sight, indeed, the white man of today who lives where they lived would have a disdain for the Algonquians. They were indigent, and happily indigent, and with no particular desire to acquire riches. Those to the north who had not come into contact with superior civilizations which spread north from the Gulf of Mexico were singularly unenterprising in making for themselves new instruments and implements. They were willing to trust in what most belonged to them : their skill as a hunter, the strong arm, the swift foot, the keen eye. The snow-shoes which they used—the well-known

Canadian racquet — were probably not their invention but that of the Dene tribes to their north, and the Algonquian birch-bark canoe may have come from a similar source. These northern Algonquians could weave baskets, and fishing-nets, make bows and arrows, build the most rudimentary of houses, igloo-shaped out of skins, or bark, but their usual method of boiling water was a sample of their lack of technical ingenuity. They first heated stones in a pile and then dropped the hot stones into some hollow stump of a tree into which they or the skies had poured water.

The Algonquians farther south — those of New England for instance — had more technical skill. They could make pottery kettles with a pointed base, like a helmet turned upside-down, which they could support by stones and then build a fire about. Also they knew how to plant maize, beans and squash, having acquired the art in a manner indicated by the legend that Roger Williams found among the Rhode Island Indians, which said that a crow from the south-west had brought to them originally the seeds of these plants.* They could also carve faces out of stone, and incise pictures, like a writing upon rock. They showed signs of having been once used to copper.

But these arts were borrowed arts, in which, if we judge by the graves, they were growing less and less skillful. In their spirit they clung to a contempt for the agricultural life. It was something tame and unmanly. They had the same kind of disdain for a sedentary people that a noble bandit in

* Roger Williams, *Key into the Language of America*, Coll. Rhode Island Hist. Soc., vol. I, p. 86.

Albania has for a storekeeper. The Algonquians were not enterprising in acquiring material wealth, nor were they tenacious in clinging to it when it fell into their hands. They were hunters : first and last hunters. And yet our second glance shows that they had riches of a kind that make us seem a bit impoverished. Their riches were fortunate riches ; they could be distributed among all, and were distributed among all. Every child of eight years old received his share, and the number of people who shared did not decrease the portion allotted to each. Each received all. And it was a heritage that could be handed on without litigation. It was the sacred traditions which the Algonquians clung to, and by which they had something of the same sense of stability that the modern man has from the ownership of land. The Algonquians clung to their sacred traditions as they clung to life itself.

To say this is not to say something that applies only to the Algonquians. The Eskimo to their north had their even more sacred traditions. The Iroquois and Sioux to the south had traditions equally sacred. All peoples have their sacred traditions, even modern industrialized nations, although it is sometimes difficult to have the perspective to see them. Especially do the peoples prize them who cannot read and write, and who preserve their traditions orally. But in the traditions of the Algonquians was something which gave them distinction. Clearly among their traditions, imbedded in them, lay the belief in a god who was more than a force of nature, more than a thunder-clap, more than an animal, more than a man,

more than an ancestor who had leaped to heaven,—"a High
God." *

The definition of such a god was not found in any "credo"
of theirs. Had a tourist gone among them in the old days
and asked them the distinct question, "Have you a High
God?" the answer would probably have been "No." The
High God of the Algonquians can be found in their ceremonies and customs that presuppose him, and in the metaphors
of their prayers and songs. From the study of such emerges a
god, called by the anthropologists a "High God." He is one
whose picture cannot be drawn. He needs nothing, can do
all, knows all. He cannot be bargained with as a spirit or
power — in the Algonquians tongues a manitu — can be bargained with.

Not all the various Algonquian tribes celebrated their High
God in the same fashion, for the various Algonquian peoples
had had very different destinies. They had not come to
North America — so the anthropologists think — in one invasion, but in several, which may have been centuries apart.
Among the Arapahoes of the West, who are held to have
belonged to a later invasion, the belief in a High God is discernible in the creation ceremonies which lasted — and still
last — eight days. In this octave the creation of the world is
symbolized, and by its rites the world is renewed. It is as if
the whole tribe were transported back to the beginning of
things. Listen to some of their praying.

* On the High God of the Algonquians see W. Schmidt, *High Gods in
North America,* Oxford, 1933.

"My Father, have pity on us! Remember that we are your children from the time you created the heaven and the earth with a man and woman, . . . We cannot cease praying to you, my Father, Man-Above, for we desire to live on this earth, which we are now about to paint on this occasion. We have given this belt to the sweet smoke for our purity hereafter. May our thoughts reach into the sky where there is holiness. Give me good water and abundance!" *

The ceremonies of the Arapaho have the mark of the West upon them. "Give me good water and abundance," they say, which suggests they must be near a desert. The Arapaho have borrowed some metaphors and dances from their neighbors the Sioux, who worship a Sun-God. In the East living originally in Pennsylvania were the Delaware or Lenapé,† Indians who showed their belief in a High God in a different fashion : most noticeably in their grand Thanksgiving Festival which lasted twelve days. This festival comes in the autumn and is celebrated in a Big Hut which represents the universe.

The word Lenapé means man — not man the hero, but man the human being. In this hut, as in the Universe, dance the Lenapé, circling round a center-post which stands for the power and solicitude of the Creator, the Great Manitu, the Great Spirit. In their formulas, in their prayers and recitations, it is evident that their Manitu not only made the world, but still cares for it. He holds the center-post in place with his own hand. He leans on it, not forgetting his children the

* G. A. Dorsey, *The Arapaho Sun-Dance*, p. 74, quoted with comment in W. Schmidt, *High Gods in North America*, p. 106.

† On this subject see M. R. Harrington, *Religion and Ceremonies of the Lenapé*, Heye Foundation, 1921.

Lenapé, not though they are separated from him by eleven skies, not though between him and man are other spirits whom he himself created : lesser manitus. And they remember him. Each year, therefore, they light once again the holy fires by means of a drill-borer in memory of the "Let there be light" of Creation.

Not all the Algonquians had the grandeur of ceremonies that the Lenapé had, who were rich among the Algonquians, having become agricultural. But all the Algonquians in one way or another recognized a Supreme Being, and generally the poorer they were the clearer to them was the conception of such a god, for he had not become associated with magic, nor with social needs. The Cree and Montaignais of northeastern Canada, the poorest of the poor, had the least tendency to identify their Manitu of Manitus with the sun or any heavenly body. Their Manitu had unforgettably created the world out of nothing. "Thou who standest," was probably his aboriginal name. He was the Master of Life, the Master of Food, the Master of Death.*

This belief in and worship of a transcendent Supreme Being gave to all Algonquians a dignity. They had the dignity of being humble, the dignity of being patient — the dignity in short of being men rather than fiendish and inhuman pseudo-angels. They were not uprooted, either, from reality, and therefore spiritually sterile. They were in contact with reality and its mystery, and had not fenced themselves from the

---

* For a discussion of the High God among the Montaignais see John M. Cooper, *The Northern Algonquian Supreme Being*, Catholic University, Anthropological Series, No. 2, 1934.

abysses of wisdom by mere formulas. They were a kind of primitive contemplative.

As such they were admired by the first White Men who saw them, even when those White Men had no desire to admire them. Captain John Smith, who had been weathered and hardened by much worldly experience, admired them. "He entertained us," says Captain John Smith, speaking of a Virginian Algonquian, "in so modest a proud fashion, as though he had been a prince of civil government, holding his countenance without laughter or any such ill behaviour. He caused his mat to be spread on the ground, where he sate down with a great majestie, taking a pipe of tobacco : the rest of his company standing about him." * Similarly the same Captain was astonished at the father of Powhatan who had "such a grave and majestical countenance as drove me into admiration to see such state in a naked savage." †

In 1603 a man of much finer spiritual perceptions than Smith made somewhat the same observations. His name was James Rosier. He was an Englishman, the agent of the Earl of Arundel, traveling as an investigator in the ship of Captain Weymouth, along the shores of Maine, where the Algonquians were less agricultural and more primitive than those of Virginia. And this is how he wrote, speaking of some Indian sachems or chiefs :

"Our Captain had two of them at supper with us in his cabin to see their demeanor, and had them in presence at service. Who behaved themselves very civilly, neither laugh-

* *Travels and Works of Captain John Smith*, ed. 1910, vol. 1, p. lxv.
† *Ibid.*, vol. 1, p. 19.

ing nor talking all the time, and at supper fed not like men
of rude education, neither would they eat or drink more than
seemed to content nature ; they desired peas to carry ashore
to their women, which we gave them, with fish and bread,
and lent them pewter dishes, which they carefully brought
home (that is back to the ship)." *

Also in our own days the human dignity of the Algonquians
continues to be praised. Father Schmidt, Professor at the
University of Vienna, who has made a particular study of
primitive religions, and who has read all that has been written
in eulogy or detraction of the Algonquians has praised them
as high examples of those who follow a noble primitive
religion :

"The prayers of the Algonkins are not mere formulae to be
recited only by the lips. The seriousness, the deep meditation,
and inner concentration of mind with which they are performed are attested by all writers. The strong inner commotion of the soul might, even with the bravest warriors, go so
far as to break out into weeping and sighing, as is illustrated,
for example, by the West Cree. Even in solemn public ceremonies, in which every motion of hand and foot is strictly
regulated by an ancient ritual, men, compelled by the strength
of their individual impulse, may transgress these regulations.

"In the great creation ceremony of the Arapaho it has
occurred that the principal officiant, representing the first
ancestor of humanity, overcome by internal commotion and
fervour, left the place rigidly assigned to him by the ancient

* *Early English and French Voyages,* editor H. S. Burrage, New York,
1930, p. 372.

ritual, approached the central post of the sacred house, which represents the Great Spirit, entwined his arms around it and called loudly and affectionately, praying to the Father above and to the Old Men of the four cardinal points to help him and his fellow dancers in their efforts to purify themselves.

"Not only the public or common, but also the individual prayer, for which they retire to solitude, is practised freely by many Algonkin tribes, for instance the Ottawa, the Cheyenne, and others, and it was employed for all possible individual needs." *

Dr. Frank G. Speck goes even farther than Father Schmidt. He describes one of the modern Lenapé, living in Oklahoma, in the following words :

"Witapanoxwe, 'Walking with Daylight,' or War Eagle, as he is known in his profession of herbalist, displays the patience, the courtesy and character of a gentleman. Representing the type once referred to by Dr. Dorsey as a natural gentleman and 'sport,' the Indian was still unspoiled by a mercenary and material civilization. He remained the simple-mannered, sympathetic, beautifully poised, contented, nature-loving, thoughtful and mystic Algonkin. He deserves more extensive personal notice, since he typifies Emerson's definition of a great man as 'one who in a crowd keeps the independence of solitude' !" †

At the same time it must not be thought that the Algonquians had the Christian religion. Their religion was not adequate. It gave them no sure rule of life, for generally

* *The High Gods in North America*, p. 81.
† Quoted in *The High Gods in North America*, p. 80.

speaking their moral code had little to do with their Supreme Being, and was based on their social needs. Neither did it give them any way of beginning their eternal life here on this earth. There is probably some truth in what the Protestant Moravian Missionary said of the Lenapé in the early eighteenth century. He called them "unspeakably indolent and slothful. They have little or no ambition or resolution; not one in a thousand of them has the spirit of a man." * Their patience, thus, their trust in a God above gods, could turn into lassitude. They did believe in a future life, and here and there recited phrases in praise of it. "Everything looks more beautiful there than here," said the Lenapé. "Everything looks new, and the waters and everything are lovely. No sun shines there, but a light much brighter than the sun : the Creator makes it brighter by its power." † But they could receive no effulgence from this future life, not on this earth as a Christian can. Therefore they disregarded it, pretty much as the Greeks did. They found their chief joy in contemplating the creation of the world, but it was not a joy which could satisfy the human heart. Their religion at its best was an unhappy blind religion.

But not only was their belief a mere glimmer of the truth, it was a glimmer that was fading; their religion was deteriorating. The simple sacrifice of first-fruits which the Algonquians had originally offered to their High God played less and less a supreme part in their lives. Either other less adequate ways were found of worshipping him, or other less

* D. H. Brinton, *The Lenapé and Their Legends*, p. 62.
† Quoted in Schmidt, *High Gods in North America*, p. 96.

adequate gods were found to be worshipped. Among the ceremonies which became over-important was the "eat-all" feast. The "eat-all" feast was a ceremony practised widely throughout North America and widely throughout the world even.   When the Algonquians had enjoyed good hunting and had secured a plentiful supply of meat, they would indulge in a feast in which all the meat had to be consumed, even if all the Indians became sick from over-eating, even if the banquet had to last for days.   Such a feast was not an eating bout, not a Roman banquet, it was a religious observance, made in propitiation to the lesser gods or lesser manitus. This superstitious ceremony, and others, flourished parasitic on the simplicity of the original Algonquian religion.

If superstitions were a sign of the sure decay of a religion, then no religion, not even the Christian religion, could survive long, for there always have been and always will be super-stitions, so long as human nature is human nature, so long as there are people with warm hearts and trivial minds.   It is not that there were superstitions among the Algonquians that meant that their noble religion was doomed.   It was that they had no way of reacting against their superstitions.   There was no authority — once superstitions were established — which could call them what they were.   There was no way for any individual to decide whether or not they were super-stitions, for unless the human intellect is given the right to put order in its theology, to write a *Summa Theologica,* then the parasites of a religion cannot be distinguished from the religion itself.   The Algonquians gave no such right to the intellect, not any more than any other primitive tribe, not

any more than practically all except Christian peoples. Thus
the Algonquians can truly be said to have been in the possession of a religion that was doomed to a slow but constant
deterioration.

Akin to superstition and tending likewise to make the
Algonquians forget their High God was magic. Superstition
leads men to do trivial and inappropriate things for a sublime
purpose. Magic is slightly different. By magic men think
they can master the spirits, or powers, of nature, but they are
not interested in doing it reverently, but merely in doing it.
Magic is not worship, any more than physical science is worship. The Algonquians were originally and even to the end
more interested in worshipping than in making the forces
of nature slave to them. They asked little of life in a material
way. What they did ask — food — they trusted to be able
to find by their own skill as hunters. Nevertheless magic did
insert itself among them, partly through the example of the
agricultural peoples about them, partly through the wiles of
certain of their number who played the part of shamans.

The shamans at their best were contemplatives. They were
not priests, for priests had to be learned. The shamans trusted
to intuition, and if they had trances, it made no difference to
those who respected them whether they were half-wits, epi-
leptics, poets or natural mystics. Presumably the shamans
had more dignity before the White Men came than after, but
even when the Dutch first came to New York they found on
Manhattan Island — of all places in the world — hermits
living, shamans, who, as the Dutchmen * said incredulously,

* See Brinton, *Lenapé*, p. 71.

pretended to live ascetic and continent. But it was almost too much to expect of human nature that shamans should remain disinterested and spiritual. Most of them, or even all of them, seemed to the first French missionaries not even devil-possessed ; they were conscious, deliberate frauds. They shook tents and pretended that spirits were doing it. They were sometimes skillful of hand like jugglers. They were more often extremely clever in being able to play on human nature. They lived an easy life in comparison with their fellows, by promising them good hunting in return for very substantial reward. Often-times the Algonquian shaman, or as he is more usually called, the medicine-man, was the chief or sachem of his group. As such he was not a contemplative at all. He was simply a very cunning man. The medicine-men diverted the attention of the Algonquians from their High God, for the medicine-man never pretended to be able to master him. They worked on the lesser gods, who promised great benefits. Why bother about the High God at all ?

While magic was making the High God less important, "lying tales" were ever tending to obscure him. By "lying tales" I mean legends which though handed on from generation to generation were not taken entirely seriously. They occupied somewhat the same relation to the truly sacred legends as fiction does to our history. It is not necessary to explain how these tales arose. The Algonquians liked the telling and making up of stories as other people do. They had long winter, northern, nights in which to tell those stories. They could not sleep all the time, nor hunt all the time. But also they had neighbors whose stories fascinated them. The Sioux had legends of a tricky god, a hare, who was the hero of many a tale. To the Sioux in some cases — particularly in the case of the Winnebagoes — the Algonquians imparted their own higher spirituality, but from the Sioux they took the mischievous legends of the hare. Farther to the south were the civilizations of Mexico and Central America. The Algonquians, who thought nothing of wandering a thousand miles, came in contact with them or, if not with them, with those who had been in contact with them. So tales of the Aztec gods found their way into their collection of "lying tales." It is surmised that the Thunder-Bird, celebrated in the legends of the Ojibways of Michigan, and incised by New England Algonquians on the rocks in the Connecticut River at Brattleboro, Vermont,* is no other than Quetzalcoatl of the Aztecs very thoroughly transformed.

What is wonderful about the Algonquians is that in spite of the fascination of these tales they kept a place in their minds for their High God. That is a feat which must always first be remembered. It speaks for their tenacity, makes us not forget their nobility and special distinction. Yet these legends usurped attention that had once been given to legends more sacred. They usurped, too, some sacredness. When the first missionaries in the seventeenth century visited the Algonquians, not a few of those missionaries took the grotesque stories concerning the tricky hare to be the most sublime myths concerning the origin of things that the Algonquians possessed. Francis Parkman making his investigations in the

* Photographs of these Thunder-Birds in Vermont can be found in C. C. Willoughby, *Antiquities of New England Indians*, Cambridge, 1935, p. 170.

nineteenth century came to the conclusion that Manabozho, or the Great Hare,* was the most conspicuous figure in Algonquian mythology. He decided that though there was some evidence of a shadowy belief in a nobler higher deity, yet to that deity no attributes were ascribed nor any worship offered.

There was only one way in which the Algonquians could cling to their High God, and that was by an uncompromising conservatism : what was oldest was best. This, indeed, they practised, but the method, though it had some success, was in itself a painful method. It bound the Algonquians to the past, turned their gaze back ever to the Creation of the World. This might in itself have been supportable, if it had not been that whatever touched the holiness of antiquity also became holy. All that was ancient was inviolable. Customs which had begun by being only of a social and material utility ended by becoming as sacred as the most sacred traditions, and they could not be pruned. They could not be criticized. There was a tendency for everything to be prescribed. There was a way to do everything. It was the way it had been done.

Fortunately the Algonquian social life was so simple, the material needs were so few, that the Algonquians lived more freely than most North American Indians. They were more individualistic. The belief in a High God freed them from worshipping what was earthly and trivial. Yet there were various "Thou Shalt Nots" among them, which may once have had some reasonableness in a social emergency, but which

* See Parkman, *The Jesuits in North America*, Boston, 1897, pp. 68-9.

had become a mere senseless bondage. In other words they had their heritage of taboos.

The bondage of taboos can be too much laughed at. A good word can be said for taboos in general, and for some of the Algonquian taboos in particular. The white colonists in New England in the seventeenth century, profited by one taboo. It was a taboo which kept the Indians from violating the wives and daughters of the colonists whom they had captured. Another of their taboos does us today some good—some good by making us think — : the young Algonquian couples newly-married did not consummate their marriage until a year after they had been formally married and had begun to associate familiarly with each other. The Algonquians near Quebec in the seventeenth century were horrified when two young Christianized Algonquians, Abenakis, became father and mother to a child within a year of their marriage. Such a taboo is not Christian, but it is religious, and the mention of it makes some people think twice, especially if they have romantic notions that the Indians were children of nature obeying their every impulse, which was just what they never obeyed, except when drunk, or in Shamanistic ecstasy. Some of the Algonquian taboos had dignity. All of them exacted a discipline. They made men men, even though they sometimes made them twisted men. Animals do not have taboos.

Yet even though the Algonquians had fewer taboos than Indians of a richer material civilization, and even though they were not so debased by taboos, as some moderns would like to think, they were by taboos enchained. Their conservatism, which preserved for them their dignity of worship, also enslaved them. And this slavery they felt and suffered from. The longing to escape from it into an individual freedom was partially satisfied by the contemplation which every Algonquian at one time or another of his life practised in order to choose for himself his tutelary manitu, and which some Algonquians practised throughout their lives, yet such contemplation was not enough for their hearts. A recourse was had to the idleness of mere reveries and dreams as if to a world more real than our waking world, in which world of dream a man was irresponsible, and where he was above and beyond the prescriptions of his ancestors. The Algonquian Indians were like all North American Indians in giving too great respect to dreams. They were also like other North American Indians in having a desire for another freedom : that acquired through the use of fire-water. Fire-water in its form of brandy, and later of rum, was the great means of escape from a past that shackled them. The readiness with which they turned to fire-water, when it was handed to them by the French, was so significant, so dire in its consequences, that it cannot be explained away by reasons that leave out of account the deep and religious cause of its existence.

The Algonquians were not then happy savages, rejoicing in a happy religion. Neither were they happy in being able to preserve their religion, such as it was. There are people nowadays in Europe and America who are losing their religion, and know they are losing it, and are not disturbed thereby, but they gain a cheerfulness, such as it is, from looking forward to an earthly prosperity, which the wonders

of the technical skill they have acquired makes them think
is no great distance off. The Algonquians had no such cheerfulness. They had but a vague spiritual hope, and no separate
material hope whatsoever. This gave them a spiritual old
age, which was in marked contrast to the youthfulness and
hopefulness of the Europeans, and made it all the more ridicu-
lous that the Europeans seeing their nakedness entitled them
babies. The Algonquians were not in bodies old men, nor
were their senses jaded, yet their minds were incredulous as
the minds of old men are incredulous. Their humor was
Oriental and sardonic. Once an Algonquian complained to
a missionary that the Christian laws were contradictory. They
forbade him, he said, to have but one wife — he had seven —
and yet forbade him to kill. How was he going to get rid
of his six extra wives without killing them? This was not
childishness. It was deliberate and terribly ungleeful irony.

The Algonquians used laughter not to exult with but to
cut. It was laughter — the laughter of public opinion — that
they most feared as the cruel enforcer of their customary law.
They were joyless and grave and patient. Of all the facile
epithets hurled at the Indians by the romancers, *stoic* has,
perhaps, the most truth of any. The Algonquians were *stoic*.
They had waited so long that they seemed to be expecting
nothing, but even then they were more than stoic. They were
the symbol of pagan patience, of the noblest of pagan patience,
that which in various primitive tribes believed still in a High
God, and waited for him to give them they knew not what.
They had become paralyzed spiritually into an impassivity

from which they could not be waked into joy, save by a help which only their High God could give, which only their High God could conceive, and which from no one but their High God they would receive.

CHAPTER III

THE IROQUOIANS

CATHERINE's father was an Iroquois and an Iroquoian. He belonged to one of the Five Nations to whom the French gave the name Iroquois. He belonged to that group of people who speak a language akin to the Iroquois nations and are thus referred to as Iroquoians.

If the map of North America, marked red where it was inhabited by Algonquians, should be painted blue where it was occupied by Iroquoians, the Iroquoian lands would look like blue islands in a red ocean, showing about as grandly as Cuba and the greater Antilles would show if they were planted in the middle of the Atlantic. As a matter of fact the blue Iroquoian islands in the red sea were not in the middle of that sea. They were toward the eastern shore of that sea, toward the eastern shore of North America. They were none the less completely surrounded by red. They were islands, small islands, drowned in Algonquians.

Nevertheless the Iroquoian lands were more of an empire than were the Algonquians even though they were isolated one from another, and even though they were not at all averse to being at war one with the other. It was not that the various islands of Iroquoians were more densely populated than the Algonquian countries and that therefore they were not inferior in numbers. The Iroquoians in spite of their denser population were always out-numbered by their neighbors. Scarcely a war did any Iroquoian nation enter into with a nation not Iroquoian but it fought at a numerical disadvantage. The Iroquoians lands were something like an empire only in that they had some kind of unity.

It was not a racial unity. Less even than the Algonquians were the Iroquoians all of one race. They were composed of long-heads and broad-heads, a mixture explained by the anthropologists as being due to the fact that a long-headed people had adopted broad-headed captives into their community.

Linguistically, however, they were so united that they were conscious of their unity. The Algonquians would never have known that they were one stock if the scientists had not told them so ; the Iroquoians could recognize their unity by finding that they could understand all Iroquoians. It was not easy, yet it could be done. No scientist had to come along to tell a Huron Indian in Canada that a Cherokee in Georgia was one of his kind. The fact that each possessed somewhat the same treasure of words revealed it.

There was a unity, also, to the culture of all the Iroquoian peoples. Superficially the unity stood out in the fact that they were all of them builders of long-houses in which to live, houses which looked like whales stranded on land, or to the French missionaries like some of the garden-arbors of the gentle land they had left behind. Whereas the Algonquians lived usually one family to a hut, the Iroquoians lived three or four families to a house. Thus the houses had to be fifty or so feet long, and could be one hundred feet long. They had shelves along the walls on which the Indians slept, and were divided into sections — one to a family — so that they bore some resemblance to modern American sleeping-cars, except that they gave no jolts, astonished with no luxury, and provided absolutely no privacy.

But the architecture of the Iroquoian long-house was not the fundamental characteristic of Iroquoian culture, any more than were the triple palisades built around their groups of long-houses as a protection. Such things could be changed as the environment changed. A thing that could not be changed among the Iroquoians was their custom of tracing descent through the mothers. The Iroquoians were matri-linear. This means not necessarily that the women ruled, although the women had rare prerogatives among the Iro-quoians. It meant more specifically that the women counted. The young man joined the long-house of his wife. His dig-nity descended through his mother. If he were elevated to a sachemship, or chieftaincy, it was by the choice of a matron, though with the consent of the men.

The tribes which belonged to the Iroquoian unity do not make anything like the list that the Algonquians make. The Algonquians were more numerous as a whole, and were broken up into smaller subdivisions. The farthest north of the Iroquoians were the Hurons, situated on Georgian Bay, an indentation of Lake Huron, on land which is part of the Province of Ontario, Canada. Southwest of them were the Erie and Tobacco Nations, which in the seventeenth century were annihilated by their fellow-Iroquoians the Iroquois.

East and south of these who were annihilated lived, in what is now New York State, those who did the annihilating. South and west of the annihilators lived, as long as the annihilators would allow it, the Andastes. Beyond them were the Tuscaroras who in the eighteenth century were allowed to consider themselves not only as Iroquoians but as Iroquois. Still farther to the south and west extended into Georgia five more tribes who are referred to as the "Five Civilized Tribes," among whom the best known is the Cherokee.

This geographic distribution must not be thought of as permanent — it was simply the distribution of Iroquoians during the first years of the seventeenth century — but it does indicate a permanent characteristic of the Iroquoians. They liked higher land than the Algonquians, not for reasons of health, but for strategic reasons. They were surrounded by hostile tribes, and they chose places where they could defend themselves, and from which they could make successful forays. The Iroquois boasted that their lands in New York State were the top of the world. Did not from it flow down the St. Lawrence River, the Hudson River, the Delaware, the Susquehanna, and the Ohio? The Five Civilized Tribes chose, until the White Men ousted them to Oklahoma, lands more visibly upland : the foot-hills of the Appalachians. The Hurons occupied a country singularly well-protected with a wonderful fish supply at its doors, and which was set on a trade-route between the Great Lakes and the Saguenay River — a back road through the Province of Quebec.

The tribe which gave its name to the Algonquians was the Algonquin tribe of Three Rivers, a tribe not necessarily the most important of the Algonquians. With the Iroquoians the case is different. They derived their name from the title given by the French to the people of the Five Nations of New York State, that is from the Iroquois. With all due regard to the Hurons or to the Andastes or to the Five Civilized Tribes, the Iroquois are superlatively the Iroquoians. By them and in them we can read the rôle played by the Iroquoians in North American history. They have been more important in determining the destinies of the United States than have any other Indian people. Their history has been more studied and more celebrated in literature than that of any other of the original inhabitants of their continent.

The knowledge that is usually possessed of them serves as a very good basis for the investigation of their culture. We all know that the Iroquois were the American Indians who established a League of Nations, and a League of Nations which worked. Five nations at first belonged to it, and then six nations. Their league had a federal government before the federal government of the United States was established. Their government governed through a congress which met annually at a capital city, the so-called Castle of the Onondagas. In this congress each nation had its representation, and — except for the late-coming Tuscaroras, the sixth nation — their vote. The decisions of the Iroquois congress had to be by nations, and had to be unanimous. The Iroquois League continued without a civil war, and faced no secession. It never really came to an end. We know all this and it is true.

We have simultaneously other knowledge which seems to

contradict this first knowledge. We know that the Iroquois were cruel. The cry of terror, "Here come the Iroquois!" echoes still through boys' books about the old Indian Wars, and echoed once through New England hills. It was uttered by the Dutch, by the French frequently, occasionally by the English of New England, and ever and ever by the Algonquian neighbors of the Iroquois. It was heard even in Europe. In the eighteenth century young bloods who wished to terrify London called themselves Mohawks, after the most famous of the Iroquois nations. The Iroquois knew the art of torture so that it is an agony to read, even in an expurgated account, what they did to their captives. They were the massacrers and torturers of the French Jesuits. And they tortured them so fearfully that even the Dutch Calvinists in pity turned pro-Jesuit — at least for the moment. They rescued Jogues, they rescued Bressani.

But how can it be that the Iroquois were so peace-loving that they formed a "league of nations," and so more than warlike that they were cruel beyond war's usual custom ? How can both of these bits of knowledge of ours be reconciled the one with the other ? Possibly some would say that the real Iroquois were the peace-makers and that the cruel Iroquois were Iroquois-not-themselves, who had been momentarily deranged in some access of rage. The Iroquois was just as real as an organizer of his league as he was in torturing his prisoners. More than that, he organized and tortured both in the same mood: a religious mood.

The reason that the peace-making and the torturing seem at first sight so incongruous one to the other is that the motive behind the peace-making is misunderstood. The parliamentary nineteenth century imagined that the Iroquois were rationalistic parliamentarians. The same century imagined that if the Iroquois were really cruel it must be because they were ogres enjoying cruelty for cruelty's sake. As a matter of fact, the Iroquois parliament had almost nothing rationalistic about it. And the Iroquois did not practise cruelties because they enjoyed them. They were not hedonists seeking perverted pleasures. They had nothing as foolish as a mere "pleasure" philosophy.

To see how the contradictions — which seem contradictions to us — can be resolved, we have to take a glance at Iroquois history. It is not a glance that can see all, but this much is evident. Iroquoians had at one time been in contact with a civilization vastly superior to their own, in wealth, in complexity, in intelligence. Where they came upon that civilization is a question in itself. They may have wandered south near Mexico, circling round over the north of Florida, where some of the tribes, it has been remarked, preserved Iroquoian words. Or it may have been that colonists from Mexico came north into the United States, and taught the Iroquois many things, and then died out or degenerated or retreated. Until the problem as to who were the mound-builders who left a huge ruined temple in Georgia, many other temples in the Mississippi Valley, and a repetition of those temples on a smaller scale as far north as Wisconsin, until that problem is solved, it is impossible to decide as to how or how not the Iroquoians came in contact with a superior culture. All that can be said surely is that it was a culture derived from Mexico, for from Mexico radiated the entire culture of the North American Indians. There was no other centre of radiation. But the point is the Iroquoians were not like the Algonquians, who mayhap touched the same civilization and, conservative, were unimpressed. They were jealous of the superior culture. They wished to preserve it, and wished to preserve the mark that it made on them.

The mark that it made on them! It is strange, as we all know, what mark a people of superior culture makes on those of an inferior one. Not always the essential things of the superior culture are imitated by those who live in the inferior. Quite the contrary : it seems as if the inessential were always copied.

What most impressed the Spaniards when they came to Mexico with Cortez was the grandeur of the civilization about them. The City of Mexico set in its lake was a magnificent Venice. The two viaducts which connected it with land were stupendous even to those who had seen the Roman viaducts of Spain. Even the commonest things in this unbelievable country had been raised to the uncommon : flutes were of gold, spindles were of gold, mirrors, hats, dishes were of gold. The magnificence showed not only in kingly palaces, but even more so in the two hundred and more temples of Montezuma's city, some of which were huge, like the pyramidal temple of the war-god Huitzilopochtli, up the one hundred and thirty steps of which Cortez marched in amazement. Everything among the Mexicans seemed grandiose, even the human sacrifices. Annually at least twenty thousand human victims were offered in the Aztec capitol. At the dedication of the great temple of Huitzilopochtli, which occurred some forty years before the Spanish conquest, seventy thousand captives had been slain.

But also the Spaniards could not help but see the intricacy of the civilization, for it was not that of a people merely rich in building materials, or drowned in mere quantity of gold. The pattern of civilization extended down to the smallest detail. All of life had its art. The goldsmiths were wonderfully skillful. So were the makers of garments out of feathers. And the priests were skillful. They were skillful in their teaching of the children, and skillful in sacrificing their victims. Nothing in this civilization was done carelessly. It was as if they were all of them living a great liturgical life in a liturgy that was at times horror itself. With what meticulous perfection was the youth prepared to be sacrificed to Tescatlipoca! Every luxury, every attention was offered him, and when he had at last come to the fatal day when he was ready for his torture, "they led him" says Prescott, "to the sacrificial stone, a huge block of jasper, with its upper face somewhat convex. On this the prisoner was stretched. Five priests secured his head and his limbs ; while the sixth, clad in a scarlet mantle, emblematic of his bloody office, dextrously opened the breast of the wretched victim with a sharp razor of itzli,— a volcanic substance — hard as flint,— and inserting his hand in the wound, tore out the palpitating heart." *

It is obvious that the Iroquois did not carry with them into the Appalachian Highlands any of the Aztec grandeur. They built no temples, no cities. All of their riches they could

* Prescott, *Conquest of Mexico,* Philadelphia, 1869, p. 76.

have carried in a pouch hung around the neck. It is fair to say that sometimes they did capture a hundred captives or more, and offer a score or two of them as a holocaust to their god, but even that could not make the Iroquoian village much like the City of Mexico.

Neither did the Iroquoians carry away with them very much of the handicraft of the Aztecs. They could carve tobacco-pipes better than the Algonquians, but they were, none of them, jewelers or metal-workers. They knew how to grow corn and squash and beans, but that was not a very striking similarity to the Aztecs, for the Aztecs though they did farm, were also commercial and military. Only two arts of the Aztecs they clung to with some dexterity. They could make feather decorations. Also they could cut out skillfully the hearts of their victims.

Truly the Iroquoians carried away from the superior civilization, which they had touched, nothing more essential than mannerisms. Some of these mannerisms had an organic relation to their existence. The treatment of their victims in war was really a part of the cult of their gods and though they may have taken those gods from Mexicans, they had made those gods their own. For the most part, however, the mannerisms were quite inorganic to the existence of the Iroquoians, and even served only to remind them that they were superior to the other people around them, and to symbolize their determination not to sink in the scale.

As a result of what they had imitated, the Iroquoians were leading a simple life in a very complex way. They were doing many, many more things that they could not justify than we who now walk in their old habitats are doing. They were like a family fallen in fortune, but not in pride and not in determination, which though it could not afford more than a morsel of bread for its banquet, yet changed its dishes ten times while eating that morsel, and afterwards swept away elaborately the crumbs when there were none.

One of the complexities of the Iroquoian culture was the system of clans. The Five Nations, the Five Civilized Tribes, the Hurons — all the Iroquoian nations, in fact — were divided into clans. Among the Iroquoians who were Iroquois, there were three clans which existed among all the Five Nations : the Bear, the Wolf, the Turtle. Other clans existed in this or that of these nations, but not in all of them. There were eight clans * in all in the Onondaga nation : the Bear, the Wolf, the Turtle, the Beaver, the Snipe, the Eel, the Deer, the Hawk. Except for the Tuscaroras, the Onondagas were the only nation which possessed an Eel Clan. Now why did these clans exist ? And why did they exist in some nations and not in others ?

L. H. Morgan, a very famous anthropologist of the nineteenth century, who collected more data than anyone else on the Iroquois, looked on the Iroquois as very deliberate statesmen, fashioning their institutions after the manner of the framers of the Constitution of the United States. He liked to find a political sagacity in all they did. To him the clans had an international function in the Five Nations. They cut

---

* There are contradictory accounts as to the number of clans in the Five Nations. This list is taken from W. W. Beauchamp, *A History of the New York Iroquois,* 1905, p. 145.

across the nations, bound the Bear Clan of the Onondagas
with that of the Mohawks, counteracted a too extravagant
nationalism, and knit together the federation in a secondary
and very skillfully devised manner. But what respect did the
Bear Clan of the Mohawks have for the Bear Clan of the
Hurons ? And within the Five Nations why did the clans
not cut across all the Nations ? The Eel Clan of the Onondagas had, until the eighteenth century, when the Tuscaroras
joined the federation, no other Eel Clan to associate with.
It is very difficult to see what international function was
played by the clans in Iroquoian society in such a state of
civilization as the White Men found them in.

Anthropologists less politically minded than L. H. Morgan
have seen a moral and social function in the clans. The clans
were exogamous, that is to say each young Iroquoian had to
marry outside of his clan, just as with us a young person mar-
ries outside of his or her immediate family. It looks as if
the clans had taken the place of the family as we know it.
The long-house among the Iroquoians was not the habitation
of a husband, and his wife, and their children. It was the
habitation of a section of a clan over which presided a matron.
If a young girl of that long-house married, her husband did
not become a member of that long-house, or anything more
than a visitor in her clan. The child she might give him
called the other children of the long-house — all of them —
sisters and brothers, and he called the men of his mother's
generation, his father included, uncles. Under such circumstances something like this exogamical regulation was neces-

sary to keep a man from marrying, among the sisters of his cabin, his real sister.

But without this division into clans there would not have been the necessity of the exogamy. Almost surely the clans were relics of a social and economic system which was distinctly not that of the Iroquois as the White Men have known them. It was, perhaps, part of a social system once possessed by the Iroquoians themselves, from which they had fallen. More likely it was a contagion which had spread from somebody else's civilization. The Aztecs had a very complicated social system with trade-guilds and castes. Possibly the clans were an attempt to copy that complexity. Or maybe another institution of the Aztecs gave an origin to the clans or was related to them.

The Aztecs of Mexico City when the Spaniards came there were divided into twenty groups [*] with their own symbols and their own military pride. These groups had nothing to do with the geography of the City of Mexico. They cut across the four well-defined quarters of the City just as the Iroquois clans cut across the Five Nations. They cut also across the three main classes of Aztec society : the nobles, common people and slaves, and across the complicated subdivisions of the common people. These twenty divisions had little organic relation to Aztec society, they were important only in parades and pageantry. In that they were very important, and would have been thought of utmost importance by a tourist. Probably these twenty divisions were them-

[*] Radin, *The Story of the American Indian*, 1934, p. 103.

selves relics of some previous condition of the Aztecs before they had descended into Mexico. It would be ironic but not impossible if the Iroquois had somehow copied from the Aztecs an institution which the Aztecs themselves had lost any real use for.

Another bit of Iroquoian culture seems to be similarly a relic of what to the Aztec was also a relic : the delight in formal speeches. Each of the clans of Mexico City had its "speaker," who was a man whose rôle had once been very glorious. When the Aztecs were conquering Mexico from the north, these speakers were the grand ambassadors who with great words demanded tribute of those whom they had conquered or intimidated. Now the conquests were over, but the grand oratory was not allowed to cease. It continued when the ambassador had turned into a prosaic tax-gatherer. It very likely was what the outlying peoples thought of as most typical of the Aztecs, and what they could best imitate in order to be civilized like the Aztecs. Many of the Algonquians and Sioux peoples of America were masters at speech-making, but the Iroquois excelled them all. Their speech-making was scarcely ever rationalistic, or directed primarily to persuasion, it was ceremonial and dramatic. It was a show of civilization.

We can laugh, if we will, at the things the Iroquoians chose to imitate from the Aztecs or from those who had visited the Aztecs, but we cannot laugh at the tenacity with which they chose to retain what they had selected. The sacred traditions of the Algonquians were not bound up with a material culture, and the Algonquians were not tenacious about maintaining arts and crafts which here and there had been thrust upon them. The Iroquoians, on the other hand, identified their religion with a material culture. They clung to the cult and the culture as inseparable. They had a tone of scorn for those about them who had not their treasure of tradition. They called their Adirondack neighbors, for instance, *bark-eaters*. They had a religious contempt for those who were not agriculturalists. They were a people with a secret, with a prosperity. They were a chosen people, surrounded by the Gentiles. Their most fundamental name for themselves was Ongwe-Owe — the only true, or the men of men.*

The Iroquoians considered as essential to their superiority that thing which they clung to with the grimmest determination. In their course northward parallel to the Atlantic Ocean, as they clove between the Algonquian peoples, they never surrendered their agricultural habits. Their social system adapted itself to giving agriculture special privileges. Even though war was the occupation of heroes, even though the mere hunting may now and again have fed their bellies better than grains of corn, yet they safeguarded their fields. In order to let them not disappear they put the women in charge of them, and, partly for that very reason, woman had a high place among them.

The relation of Iroquoian women to Iroquoian agriculture is not something to be passed over lightly. It was not a scarcity of labor that set the women as workers in the field

---

* See Arthur C. Parker in Chapter on "Iroquois," *History of State of New York*, vol. 1, 1933.

and consequently as patrons of it. Neither was it the lazi-
ness of the men that forced a servile work upon them. To
be agricultural was the mark of an Iroquoian superiority. The
Algonquians, who did not understand its mystery, were inferior. When the Europeans first came on the Iroquoians,
they found that the Iroquoians had the habit of making winter hunts. Now the Iroquoians on these hunts felt that they
were least Iroquoian. Their social rules were associated particularly with their village and their long-houses. Therefore they lived much more freely in the woods than they did
at home. Often they took other women for wives, temporary
wives, which was not frowned on, for on the hunting expedition the Iroquoian was scarcely an Iroquoian. His days on
the hunt did not count. Only if the taking of the extra wife
had lowered the prestige of the real wife would the hunting
custom have aroused opposition. As a matter of fact it did
not. The real wife had merely to be the real wife when she
was in the village, near to the civilization of the Iroquoian
over which she had trusteeship. Her high position stayed with
her so long as there was a store-house within the palisades of
her town, and just outside those palisades a field for next
spring's planting, and next fall's harvest.

It was not due entirely to their connection with agriculture
as a superior activity, however, that the women had a superior
place among the Iroquois. They were superior also because
where at all costs a contact with the past had to be maintained, women were the surest links with it. Descent could
with certainty be traced through a mother. Therefore the
Iroquois were matrilinear. But also traditions could be more

safely handed down through them, for women were more conservative. Also they had the ear of the children : they told them the first stories, sang them the first songs.

The Iroquois warrior had many traits which, we might suppose, would have made him look down on women. He had an enormous pride in his courage and delight in his martial exploits. Women in such things did not count, and those of his sex whom he despised in war he called "women," yet more important than war was the perpetuation of his tradition. War-chiefs were not nearly as important in his eyes as peace-chiefs, some of whom might even be womanly. The women, the real women, were really more important than peace-chiefs. They stood for perpetuity. Only a woman could take from the torture platform a victim and save his life ; she could adopt him. When the French trader Radisson * was a captive doomed to die among the Mohawks, a sachem pleaded in his favor. He was so vehement, so dramatic, that throwing off his clothes and nearly naked he stood all of a sweat, but his words had little effect. It was the word of the sachem's wife that counted, "Come with me, my son." The women were not only the guardians of the art of agriculture, they were the guardians of the ceremonies and mannerisms which the Iroquois associated with the art of agriculture. As such they were not looked down upon, they were looked up to, even by the proudest of warriors.

The affection that the Iroquoians had for their traditions not only led them to respect women though women were

* To read how Radisson was twice saved by an Iroquois matron, see Radisson's *Voyages*, Prince Society, Boston, 1905, p. 39 and pp. 58-9.

weak, but it filled them with a deep reverence for their ancestors even though those ancestors could help them no more.
They prized their ancestors, not because of their individual
sanctity or heroism but because of their relation to the traditions which taken together were holy, were the tradition.
They were the links which enabled the tradition to be preserved. The Iroquoian of the new generation wished, therefore, to unite himself to those which had gone before. Thus
the chiefs — the peace-chiefs, who had the real prestige — were
chiefs who had inherited a name, like a magic robe, and who
from that robe derived their prestige. No great exploit could
make an Iroquois a sachem, or chief.

At the time of the American Revolution there lived among
the Iroquois of the Five Nations a statesman, scholar, and
warrior, who received from White People during his life
more recognition than any other Indian has ever received.
He was a Mohawk with an Indian name which is translated
into English as "Two-Sticks-Tied-Together," but it is as
Joseph Brant that he is generally remembered. Joseph Brant
went to England and there had his picture painted by Rom-
ney. He was adulated at the Court of George III, somewhat
as Franklin shortly previous to that had been adulated at the
Court of Louis XVI. Later he had a town named after him
in Canada, and a statue in that town erected to him. But not
only was he esteemed by the whites he was also esteemed by
his fellow-Iroquois. Joseph Brant was a remarkable man.
Yet the Mohawks were horrified when it was suggested by the
White Men that Joseph Brant be made a sachem. No individual greatness could make a man a sachem. It could make

him a war-chief, yes, but that was different. Great as was Joseph Brant, he was as nothing in comparison with a real sachem who bore a name that did not die, one that he assumed from his predecessor, one that made him (no matter how great a fool he happened to be or become) a veritable voice of the Iroquoians, the mouth-piece of a thousand generations, speaking for the past, present and future with a wisdom higher than an individual's.

The Iroquoians tried to be their own ancestors. They tried to make their past history their present history. They honored therefore their ancestors as still living in them. Also they commiserated them as having died before them, and in so doing formed another bond with the past. They mourned, to begin with, the death of each sachem, and made a great mystical event of the raising of a successor to his name. The Five Nations whose entire population was twenty thousand had fifty sachems. When any of these sachems died, a condolence ceremony took place which became an event as important in their Iroquoian lives as the coronation of a king is important in the lives of modern Englishmen. Other events, other considerations, had to wait on it. Among the several hundred thousand Iroquoians of North America there were, judging by their proportion among the Five Nations, at least five hundred sachems. Not every Iroquoian was interested in the death of every sachem, yet neither was the death of a sachem a purely national affair. Embassies had to be sent from neighboring tribes. Elaborate week-long speech-making had to be performed. Time, which was not yet called money, had to be spent, and much wealth too was lavished with it in the giving of gifts. It must have seemed at times to the Iroquoians that they were living one long condolence festival, and in verity they were.

Aside from their mourning for what was lost in the death of their friends, they had a cult for what was left behind by the deaths of those friends, their friends' bodies. Both the Algonquian and Iroquoian peoples looked forward, though dimly, to a future life, as is indicated by the phrase "happy hunting ground," which we give somewhat indiscriminately to the picture of a future existence in the minds of no matter what Indians. The Iroquois looked forward, indeed, not so much to a hunting ground as to a dancing ground, but they did look forward. At the same time they never attempted to formulate the relation of soul to body in anything except myths and metaphors. The bodies of their dead were merely a part of their ancestors that death could not take. They had buried those bodies, and they knew where they lay. Those bodies were precious and dear.

Every ten years, therefore, they celebrated a feast which among the Iroquois was the greatest of all their feasts, the Festival of the Dead. It was an act of honor paid to the bodies of those who had died during the last ten years. The bodies were disinterred, carried to a central burying ground, and there put once again into the ground, all in a common pile into which had been thrown the richest of Iroquois riches, furs, wampum — whatever was most prized.

It is not necessary to try to derive this feast from any half-understood Mexican feast. It was the spontaneous expression of the love of the Iroquois for their ancestors, for whom and in whom they were leading their lives, and enduring their hardships. It took its particular form of expression from the necessity which the Iroquois faced, of, every ten years, for reasons of public health, changing their village site. They did not wish to leave their dead. Hence this act of love. The Jesuit missionaries, even though they lamented the superstition of these rites, were deeply moved by the genuine affection shown in them. Saint Jean de Brébeuf recounts the pathetic spectacle of the digging up and carrying to new sepulchres of the bones of those lately dead. He described it as he saw it among the northernmost Iroquoians, the Hurons, in 1636. And these are his words :

"I admired the tenderness of one woman toward her father and children ; she is the daughter of a chief who died, at an advanced age, and was once very influential in the country ; she combed his hair and handled his bones, one after the other, with as much affection as if she would have desired to restore life to him ; she put beside him his Asatonewar, that is, his package of Council sticks, which are all the books and papers of the Country. As for her little children, she put on their arms bracelets of wampum, and glass beads, and bathed their bones with her tears ; they could scarcely tear her away from these, but they insisted, and it was necessary to depart immediately. The one who bore the body of this old Captain walked at the head ; the men followed, and then the women, walking in this order until they reached the pit." *

* Thwaites, vol. x, p. 293.

Similarly he described with admiration the generosity of the Iroquoians : their giving their wealth to the dead, instead of snatching it from them.

"Our savages are not savages as regards the duties that nature constrains us to render to the dead ; they do not yield in this respect to many nations much more civilized. You might say that all their exertion, their labors, and their trading, concern almost entirely the amassing of something with which to honor the Dead. They have nothing sufficiently precious for this purpose; they lavish robes, axes and porcelain (i.e., wampum) in such quantities that, to see them on such occasions, you would judge that they place no value upon them ; and yet these are the whole riches of the country." *

After reading Saint Jean de Brébeuf's description of the devotion of the Hurons to their dead, we can scarcely help exclaiming of them and of the Iroquoians in general, what some other Jesuit missionary exclaimed —"These people lived for their dead."

Living for the dead was generous, but it had its inconveniences to a people who had to fight for their existence against hostile living neighbors. Granted that the cult of the dead warmed them, and gave them a courage not their own, also it hampered them, for it oppressed them with a weight of customs and preoccupied them with a plethora of ceremonies, which indeed they enjoyed, but which kept them from other pressing affairs.

At about the time when Columbus came to America the

* Thwaites, vol. x, p. 265.

wedge of Iroquois people which had been driving northward along the Appalachians through the Algonquians arrived at the St. Lawrence River and spread down its northern bank to Quebec, and down its southern bank to the Gaspé Peninsula. The importance of the St. Lawrence River to the Algonquians was both that of a compass, for it pointed like a cartographer's line almost straight from the Great Lakes to the sea, and that of a smooth and spacious road. To the Iroquoians it was even more important. It was a path for them for two purposes, for hunting expeditions, and for commerce. The Iroquoians had some usefulness to their neighbors in that they could sell them parched corn and keep them alive when they were starving. Also the banks of the St. Lawrence were to them a fertile field. The Iroquoians coveted the St. Lawrence.

When Jacques Cartier arrived from France in 1535 and sailed up the St. Lawrence River as far as Montreal he found the Iroquoians in control of that stream which they so much coveted. There were signs that the Algonquians resented this occupation. There was already war. But in that war, the Iroquoians, although they must have been outnumbered, were holding their own.

Before Champlain, however, arrived in Canada, some seventy years later, the situation had changed. For some reason, which we shall never know, which may have been a matter of private quarrel, or may have been the sudden desire which the Algonquians had acquired of wanting to trade with the French and Spaniards and Portuguese at the mouth of the

St. Lawrence and thus acquire kettles and hatchets in return for furs, the Algonquins became fiercer in their wars, and forced the Iroquoians to retreat.

The Iroquoians were now in a dangerous predicament. There was no danger of their being exterminated : the Algonquians did not exterminate. But they might be drowned in Algonquians, and become dragged down — which they absolutely dreaded — to the level of the Algonquians. In their fight with the Algonquians they needed all their hands free for the conflict. Condolence ceremonies, and other elaborate ceremonies were tying their hands. The Iroquoians were like sailors in a storm in a heavily laden ship. If they jettisoned none of the cargo they were surely lost, if they jettisoned it all there was no use in being saved. It seemed as if the Iroquoians retreating from the St. Lawrence would have to lose either their past, or their future.

In this dilemma some of the Iroquoian nations took a step which has made the Iroquois name famous ; they established what we call the "League of the Five Nations," and what they called "The People of the Long-House." Only the vaguest and most contradictory reports tell us when this great "Long-House" was established, this Commonwealth. It may have been originated before Cartier found the Iroquoians still supreme on the St. Lawrence ; or it may be considered as something that happened after the visit of Cartier. But it had nothing whatsoever to do with copying the French, and just as surely it was caused by a crisis in warfare with the Algonquians. And above all, it was no fiction. It most emphatically did come into being, and during the seventeenth century was all too manifest. It showed itself then as an offensive and defensive alliance between five Iroquoian nations who inhabited New York State, from west to east : the Senecas, the Cayugas, the Onondagas, the Oneidas, the Mohawks. Their long-house extended from Buffalo to Albany. They were not numerous. They could not muster more than three thousand warriors, but they were extraordinarily effective. They were clever, courageous, and they clung together. They were more than an alliance. They were a federation. They had a federal government, a capital, and a definite though unwritten constitution.

It may be asked, who was the statesman behind this League ? And what was his philosophy ? We have no written record to consult. All that we can learn must be interpreted from a legend, which can be treated neither as mere fiction, nor as a chronicle, but as history spiritualized. The hero of the legend has the name Hiawatha, and was the real Hiawatha from whom Longfellow unwittingly stole the name to confer it on an Ojibway character to whom it did not belong. Hiawatha was a man with tears in his heart, as the Iroquois phrase went, a mourner for the death of his daughters, and for the calamities of his people. From another Onondaga — for Hiawatha was an Onondaga — he had learned to dream of a happier order of things in which all the Iroquoians could live under a single tree of peace. The Onondaga from whom he learned these dreams was Dehanawidah, but there was another Onondaga who had nothing but contempt for these schemes. His name was Adodarhoh, and he was the powerful pessimistic sachem of the Onondagas. Because of this latter sachem's opposition, Hiawatha had to flee to the Mohawks, but finally after five years of speech-making he accomplished something. Of the ten nations whom he wished to gather under his tree of peace he gathered together five. Hiawatha's brain did not conceive of the League of the Five Nations, but his tongue did bring the League into being. He can be called its founder.

Such a legend has given many people the impression that Hiawatha was a progressive statesman of the kind that the nineteenth and eighteenth centuries saw so many of, who wished to emancipate his people from the king-trodden past and from priest-ridden superstition. It must be acknowledged that Hiawatha did show some of the abilities of nineteenth century parliamentarians. He was good at dickering. Each of the five nations who joined the league was jealous of its own rights, and he arranged a compromise that suited them all. The Cayugas were not a numerous nation, but they were given the privilege of sending ten sachems to the Grand Council. The Onondagas had fourteen representatives there. The Senecas were twice as numerous as any of the other nations yet their representatives were but eight, and their satisfaction had to come from a privilege of another nature, that of leadership in war. The Mohawks had nine sachems at the Council; the Oneidas the same number. In making a hundred petty adjustments of this kind, Hiawatha showed himself a parliamentarian, but really he did not belong to the eighteenth century "enlightenment."

Hiawatha was trying to conserve the past, not step away from it. To a people who were in danger of throwing away

all their traditions as an intolerable load, or at least of letting
their traditions gradually fade out — as they were tending to
do among the Hurons who refused to join the league — to
such a weary people he revived the possibility of keeping their
ancient customs, by trimming them somewhat, so that they
were less impossible to be borne. In the Five Nations the
length of time given to "condolence ceremonies" was diminished, but only in order that condolence ceremonies might
continue to exist. The whole purpose of the peace which the
League brought about among the Five Nations who listened to
Hiawatha, was not that there should be a life of material comfort and uninterrupted earthly security ahead for those Five
Nations, but in order that they might be able to withstand
the outsiders, and preserve their treasure of a past.

Here is how the Five Nations sang as they came together
for their condolence ceremonies :

> "*I come again to greet and thank the League ;*
> *I come again to greet and thank the kindred :*
> *I come again to greet and thank the warriors :*
> *I come again to greet and thank the women.*
> *My forefathers,— what they established,—*
> *My forefathers,— hearken to them.*" *

The Iroquois were not trying to establish anything new or
untraditional.

The conservative nature of Hiawatha's reforms are hinted
at in the very legend which recounts them, for the story of

---

* *The Iroquois Book of Rites,* ed. Horatio Hale, Philadelphia, 1833, p. 123.

Hiawatha is like an echo of previous heroic stories, and even recalls the primal story of the culture-hero such as we find it in Mexico. Adodarhah, the Onondaga sachem, has a strange likeness to Quetzalcoatl, the old Mayan deity whom the Aztecs in their turn gave a place to. Adodarhah,* the name, means "The Entangled One," and whatever the name Quetzalcoatl may mean, the deity to whom it was applied was in graven image an entangled one, with the body of a serpent and the plumes of the quetzal bird. Quetzalcoatl had among the Mayans been a supreme deity though not as a High God : he had been a culture hero deified. When the Aztecs arrived he found himself confronted with the Aztec deity, Tezcatlipoca, who conquered yet did not dethrone him. This is almost exactly what Hiawatha did to the Onondaga sachem. Moreover the Onondaga sachem wore his feathers like the Mayan deity, and the very name Hiawatha signifying "He Who Combs Out the Hair" suggests that Hiawatha was the one who combed out the wrath from the plumed Adodarhah. Hiawatha was not looked on by the Iroquois as one who separated them from their past. In order to explain him and celebrate him, they merged him into their epic tradition, even as the Balkan bards have merged the deeds of Achilles, who lived some thousand years B.C., with those of Kraleyvitch Marco, who lived in the fifteenth century, and those of General Franchet d'Esperey, who planned the victorious artillery barrages in 1918.

A consideration of the Grand Council of the Iroquois Five Nations leads us to a similar conclusion as to the conservative

---

* Paul Radin, *The Story of the American Indian*, p. 277, New York, 1934.

nature of Hiawatha's reforms. It is quite true that the Grand
Council was very important : it assured the peace between
five nations who had hitherto quarreled among themselves,
and who would have been submerged in the Algonquians
about them had they continued to quarrel. The Council
brought peace among them, and victory to them. But the
Council was nothing unprecedented. All that was unprecedented about it was the way it worked, and its working was
made possible by the crisis in which it was created.

The Council did make decisions : each nation voted as a
unit, and the decisions in order to be decisions had to be unanimous. All of this may sound as if the Council were some
kind of a parliament. It should be remembered that the
Iroquois had no written laws, and that they promul-
gated no statutes. The Council assured that peace or war
should be made collectively by the five nations, but really it
did not declare war, nor make peace. The military chiefs
of the Iroquois, who had no vote in the Council, not, that is,
simply as military chiefs, and who had no seat in it
unless they were sachems — which by no means generally they
were — could always make war when they wanted to. War
began automatically if certain things were done against the
enemy, and those things might be done by one irresponsible
Iroquois. Public opinion alone could control that Iroquois.

All that the Council did, therefore, was to ratify what had
happened. Its coming together bound all nations to face
with one front the foe before them. Much oratory, much
drama went on at the gatherings, but practically no cool ra-
tional discourse. The irrational character of the speeches is be-

trayed in the manner in which the women found representation there. The man who spoke for them did not confine himself merely to giving their arguments, he spoke with their voice, that is with an assumed falsetto, a woman's voice. With little exaggeration it could be said that all the sachems were play-acting, though in a very holy drama. The sachem who was now Hiawatha talked for Hiawatha. The sachem who was now Adodarhah, talked for that "tangled one." Little deliberation went on in the Annual Council. None of that planning, which was most astute of the Iroquois, their military planning, was discussed there. War strategy had nothing to do with the Council.

The true nature of the Council can well be illustrated by the account which Lewis H. Morgan has presented us of the opening of its sessions. Since Morgan, living in the last century, allowed himself to consider the Iroquois Grand Council as more like the Parliament of Westminster than any anthropologists would now concede, his description has a special authority : it is the testimony of a man who tells the truth even against his own dear theories.

"At the day appointed the sachems of several nations, with their followers, who usually arrived a day or two before and remained encamped at a distance, were received in a formal manner by the Onondaga sachems at the rising of the sun. They marched in separate procession from their camps to the council-grove, each bearing his skin robe and bundle of fagots, where the Onondaga sachems awaited them with a concourse of people. The sachems then formed themselves into a circle, an Onondaga sachem, who by appointment acted as master of

the ceremonies, occupying the side toward the rising sun. At
a signal they marched round the circle, moving by the north.
It may be here observed that the rim of the circle toward the
north is called the 'cold side' (o-to-wa-ga) ; that on the west
'the side toward the setting sun' (ha-ga-kwas-gwa) ; that on
the south 'the side of the high sun' (en-de-ih-kwa) ; and that
on the east 'the side of the rising sun' (t'ka-gwit-kas-gwa).
After marching three times around on the circle single file,
the head and foot of the column being joined, the leader
stopped on the rising sun side, and deposited before him his
bundle of fagots. In this he was followed by the others, one
at a time, following by the north, thus forming an inner circle
of fagots. After this each sachem spread his skin robe in
the same order, and sat down upon it, cross-legged, behind his
bundle of fagots, with his assistant sachem standing behind
him. The master of ceremonies, after a moment's pause,
arose, drew from his pouch two pieces of dry wood and a
piece of punk with which he proceeded to strike fire by
friction. When fire was thus obtained, he stepped within the
circle and set fire to his own bundle, and then to each of
the others in the order in which they were laid. When they
were well ignited, and at a signal from the master of the ceremonies, the sachems arose and marched three times around
the Burning Circle, going as before by the north. Each
turned from time to time as he walked, so as to expose all
sides of his person to the warming influence of the fires.
This typified that they warmed their affections for each other
in order that they might transact the business of the council
in friendship and unity. They then reseated themselves each

upon his own robe. After this the master of the ceremonies,
again rising to his feet, filled and lighted the pipe of peace
from his own fire. Drawing three whiffs, one after the other,
he blew the first toward the zenith, the second toward the
ground, and the third toward the sun. By the first act he
returned thanks to the Great Spirit for the preservation of his
life during the past year, and for being permitted to be present
at this council. By the second he returned thanks to his
Mother, the Earth, for her various productions which had
ministered to his sustenance. And by the third, he returned
thanks to the Sun for his never-failing light, ever shining upon
all. These words were not repeated, but such is the purport
of the acts themselves. He then passed the pipe to the first
upon his right toward the north, who repeated the same ceremonies, and then passed it on to the next, and so on around
the burning circle. The ceremony of smoking the calumet
also signified that they pledged to each other their faith, their
friendship and their honor." *

In truth the Iroquois League was not like a civil state of
the nineteenth century at all. It was more like a church —
a fiendish, a counterfeit church, but a church. That it was
called the "Long-House" suggests this to our minds. It was
a group of men gathered together in a body who were more
important as a body than they were as a mere collection of
individuals. They had a treasure of rites and ceremonies
which spelled to them salvation. Although these rites were
closely associated with a standard of living — an agricultural
culture — the Long-House of the Iroquois was not only a

* L. H. Morgan, *League of the Iroquois*, 1901, New York, p. 231.

church of this earth, or of those who were at any moment
alive. Symbolically the Long-House stood for the solidarity
and exclusiveness of the Iroquoians. The dead were included
in it, the Iroquois dead. After the American Revolution, after
George Washington had died, the Iroquois in gratitude to a
man whom curiously enough (to our thinking) they called
"The Destroyer of Cities," * wished to take him into their
Iroquois heaven. Much as they wanted to, they found that
by their traditions they could not. It was not that his race
kept him out. White Men alive could be adopted into the
Iroquois Long-House, could be as it were baptized, could be
given an Iroquois name. The majority of Iroquoians had
ceased to be of Iroquoian stock. But George Washington
had not shared their treasure. He had not entered their
Long-House. Therefore in the next world he could not have
the privileges of the Long-House. In their difficulty the Iroquois invented for him just outside their dancing-ground of
happiness a trim elegant estate like Mount Vernon, in which
"The Destroyer of Cities" could walk about and be, if not of
them, in view of them.†

The gods whom the Long-House worshipped were many
gods. They were okis, and some of the okis were such as we
can laugh at — mere animals to whom a personality had been
given — and others were tremendous, like the god of thunder,
the god of the sea. They came from many sources : some
were deified heroes, some were the sun and moon, some may

* It should be remembered that General Washington did in 1779 send
General Sullivan against the Iroquois and through that General burned
forty villages and destroyed 160,000 bushels of corn.
† L. H. Morgan, *League of the Iroquois*, p. 171.

have stepped out of legends that tried to explain the origin of evil and death, some had been adopted from their neighbors. In worshipping their gods the Iroquoians referred even to a highest oki,* who can be considered as a primitive High God not yet forgotten.

But this High God did not give a unity to their religion as it did to that of the Algonquians. He was too dimly discerned, his pre-eminence was not emphasized. The legends of the Iroquois did not so clearly as those of the Algonquians go back to the creation. They were obsessed with the problem of evil, and began with the great warfare between the good and the bad. The primal peace had been forgotten.

Some scholars have tried to find a unity in the Iroquois religion in ascribing to it the cult of an irrational, anonymous force, of which all the okis or manitus partook and to which the Iroquois tried in one way or another to have access : the Iroquoian orenda. Fascinating as the theory is, it can scarcely obliterate the Iroquoian polytheism, so clearly attested to by witness after witness. The Iroquois never made logical order in their gods any more than did the Greeks. Neither did they find any hierarchical order in them. The unity of the Iroquois religion was based on its value to them. It was their treasure, bound to them in an Iroquois way. It was their property : the property of the Long-House.

Among the Iroquoian gods one of the most important was Areskoi, who has been likened to the Mars of the Greeks, and to the Huitzilopochtli of the Aztecs. He or she — for the

* Morgan held that they clearly worshipped a Supreme Being.

sex of the deity could not in the Iroquoian tongues be easily determined — was a war-god, the patron of the Iroquoian church insofar as it was a church militant. Areskoi was danced to in the War Dance. To Areskoi the Iroquoians offered up their bodily sufferings, those voluntarily inflicted on themselves, and those inflicted by their enemies. To Areskoi they offered up the sufferings of their victims.

The captives of the Iroquois were not merely brutalized as an unfortunate boy can be by bullying school-mates. They were respected by their own tormentors. Radisson tells how when he was on the way to being sacrificed his head was anointed, his face ceremonially painted. Saint Isaac Jogues tells how when he was led to the Mohawk village of Ossernenon there to suffer his week of torture, he was offered with prayers to the sun-god, that is to Areskoi. This did not in the least restrain any of the cruelties, for the cruelties were themselves holy. As we know from a hundred accounts, the Iroquois captive was, unless saved by a matriarch and adopted into the nation, most fiendishly used. He had first to run a gauntlet, as it is called, which is really the walking slowly through a double row of men and women who whipped him as he passed, often with eel-skins stuffed with rock. Then he had to perform on a platform and be systematically mutilated. Finally a slow-burning took place, which ended with the tearing out of the victim's heart, and the devouring of it. The Iroquois cruelties were a prescribed religious ceremony.

It is almost impossible not to connect these ceremonies

with the Aztecs, and to imagine that they were derived from
Aztec ceremonies. Huitzilopochtli delighted in sham battles
which were nothing else than war-dances — for the war-dances
were sham battles. Huitzilopochtli was thirsty for prisoners
to be sacrificed to him. The victims among the Aztecs had
usually their hearts torn out, and like the victims of the
Iroquois were made to perform on a scaffold. In some of the
rites they were tied to posts and shot at with arrows. The Iroquois, it would seem, were remembering the Aztecs.

But also these terrible Iroquoian ceremonies can be connected with all mankind, for they have to do with suffering
in general, and its awful significance. The Iroquoians in their
fiendish way gave it a high place. The Jesuit missionary
was all admiration when an Iroquois boy of ten sang a death-
song, when a kettle of boiling water was spilled on him. Not
a word of complaint, not a whisper came from him. It was
usual for other young boys voluntarily to vie with one another
in bearing pain without murmuring, for instance, in putting
red-hot embers under the arms. Pain was something not
merely for others to suffer. Nor was it for those who chose
to suffer it merely a salutary discipline, hardening one for
war. It was a sacrifice. Somehow it made people greater
than they ordinarily were, as those were made greater by
eating the heart of the victim that had suffered. In one case —
if we are to believe Radisson — an Iroquois stepped to the
platform where the victim, Radisson himself, was performing,
and between him and Radisson inserted a burning brand,
burning himself as it burned Radisson. We can never find
in the Iroquoians a theology of suffering, but we can find

everywhere among them, a pre-occupation with it, which in itself unites them to all human beings, and an awe of it, which is likewise not unusual.

The Iroquois Long-House had its humane aspect. To be kind to the feeble therein was one of its precepts. The Iroquois were bidden to care for their aged in a manner quite different from the usually less cruel Algonquians. The Algonquians when there was no way out of it killed the aged, in order to be able to hunt, to move and to live. Such a custom was not tolerated among the Iroquois, but even then the Iroquoian cruelty must not be looked on as anything incongruous to the Iroquois and their league, nor as a departure, unfortunate, from their fundamental code, as sins are among Christians. The Iroquois cruelty depended on the Long-House, and the Long-House on the cruelty. It was very nearly the cult proper of this League of Nations.

What a contrast there is, then, between the Algonquians and the Iroquoians! The former were almost quietests. They waited for God to help them. God was omnipotent. They were powerful only to thank him, whether he gave them what they wanted or did not want. They were good hunters, and were not averse as such to using the skill which belonged to them as men, but more than men they did not care to be. The Iroquois, on the other hand, wished to be gods. By owning a precious treasure of traditions, and by binding themselves into a sacred body — a church — they wished to be more than men. They, if the Algonquians trusted in God and were patient, trusted not only in their gods, but in their own efforts. They were impatient to help

themselves, were eager. To the eye of the European colonist
who looked on the Iroquoian or the Algonquian as an equal
inconvenience in his path, and who could not see that the
manner of dress, nor the manner of finding his food of the
one differed much from that of the other, the Iroquoians
and the Algonquians were scarcely to be distinguished. But
the eye, which penetrated deeper to their minds, saw that
though they were superficially the same, and wore somewhat
the same costume, and paddled somewhat the same canoes,
they were striving for utterly different goals. They were
playing in the drama of North American history utterly different parts. They served, indeed, as examples of how different human beings could be. They provided a contrast which
a human playwright would be very glad to invent. The
Algonquians would accept what Heaven sent them ; the Iroquoians would storm Heaven.

In one respect, however, they were similar. They were each
playing a tragic part. They were each, to begin with, losing
their treasure of traditions. We have seen how the Algonquians were losing theirs. It is not so easy to see how the
Iroquoians were approaching a similar failure, for we make
the mistake of thinking of their treasure as military success,
of which they gained a great deal. During the second part
of the seventeenth century the twenty thousand Iroquois of
New York State exerted a supremacy over all other Indians
east of the Mississippi from Florida to Labrador. Morgan
was so dazzled by their success that the Iroquois to him were
success itself. Had not the White Men interfered, he thought,
they would have established a kind of Aztec Empire over

the eastern half of the North American continent. But underneath the superficial success the Iroquois were failing. What they were trying to guard was their traditions, and their victories did little good to their traditions. All their victories were to them defensive victories, but each defensive victory made the next one more difficult. It destroyed a certain number, at least, of real Iroquois who had to be replaced by members of other tribes, some of them, to be sure, Iroquoians, but many of them Algonquians. These outsiders might be as able warriors as those they replaced, but they could not protect as well the treasure of the Five Nations, for they did not own that treasure. The treasure disappeared with the death of the best warriors. No wonder there grew up among the Five Nations a special class, "Keepers of the Faith," who could really remember the ways of the Iroquois. The Iroquois material culture, their technical and agricultural skill, was declining. The Iroquois discipline was declining. The magic of the medicine-men was growing. The victories were hastening the decline.

This failure to be able to cling to what they cherished was in itself tragic, but it was not nearly so tragic as the deeper tragedy which we also noted in the case of the Algonquians : even their success in preserving their treasure was a tragedy, for it was not the treasure they took it to be. We see in the Iroquois a people with a high sense of honor, who sometimes killed themselves simply because they felt they had not acted up to Iroquois standards, who devoted tremendous efforts to the preserving of a superiority over their neighbors : a superiority not purely material, but bound up with a material culture. Even when they enjoyed that culture, however, in its fulness, even when they tasted what spiritually went with it, they drank no "torrent of delight" such as flows from Christian skies. They underwent a real asceticism, but it was one which did not free them, it opened no Heaven. The Iroquoians bound themselves by a hundred bonds of etiquette that the Algonquians, more individualistic, knew nothing about. To the Iroquois the very manner of speaking was elaborate with laws and civilities, the breaking of which were a serious offense against the sacredness of what was Iroquois. To the Iroquois every move, not only in his dance but in his life, was prescribed. He bore the burden manfully — a much greater burden than the Algonquians bore — but was it worth the bearing ? In his haste to be greater than he was, he had established on earth a church of his own, but it was most certainly not God's church, nor was the service of its deities perfect freedom.

Even the Iroquoians themselves felt this. Their human nature revolted. Much more than the Algonquians did they turn to dreams. In dreams they could be individual and free. Rooted in their religion there may have been some respect for dreams, but the bondage to dreams that the Iroquois wished on themselves was even a destroyer of their religion, so did it exalt dreams. Saint Jean de Brébeuf wrote of the Hurons :

"They have a faith in dreams which surpasses all belief ; and if Christians were to put into execution all their divine inspirations with as much care as our savages carry out their dreams, no doubt they would very soon become great saints.

They look upon their dreams as ordinances and irrevocable decrees, the execution of which it is not permitted without crime to delay." *

Dreams were bad enough, but even they were not sufficient to give the Iroquoians the illicit freedom that they tried to discover, and possess. Brandy had to be summoned to the aid of dreams to give to the Iroquois a still madder and more irresponsible ecstasy. It is absolutely necessary to remember that the Iroquoians were not an undisciplined people. The drunkenness which they let the White Men force upon them was not accepted by them as men who could not control themselves, when they wished to. Iroquois went to war with no greater baggage train than a pouch of charred corn worn at their belts. They were willing to pass weeks in semi-starvation without a murmur. They were masters of themselves. And yet with all this self-restraint they ran to liquor as a man crazed with thirst does to water. When we read what the French missionaries later on wrote against the liquor traffic, we might suspect that they were fanatics of the prohibitionist sort. Their pictures of whole Iroquois villages turned into bacchanalian hilarities, and then into something filthier, and finally into a living cemetery of drunkards that could not wake for two days, might seem to be the oratory of such zealots. Yet the Jesuits were no more prohibitionists than most Frenchmen are now prohibitionists. They simply came upon and were startled by an extraordinary paradox. Here were proud men, proud women, and proud children, who could brave the terrors and sufferings of war, and the prospect

* Thwaites, vol. x, p. 169.

of death unflinchingly, and yet who could not stand the mere prospect of day-in-day-out Iroquois life, and would ignominiously drown themselves in the oblivion brought in a brandy keg.

Both the Algonquians and the Iroquoians were old peoples, who had been waiting a long time. To those who think clearly, it has always been evident from Adam's day through Virgil's to ours, that human life as we know it stands on an inclined plane : if we halt or are not supported, we slide down, for the slope to Avernus is really a slope. On this inclined plane the Algonquians were as if clinging to a tree which was slowly giving way. They were patient, apathetic, making as little effort as possible like one who in such a predicament does not wish to weaken the roots of the tree to which he is holding. On the other hand the Iroquoians were racing upwards on a landslide which descended under them. Most people prefer to cheer the Iroquois. There is more pathos to their efforts.

CHAPTER IV

THE ARRIVAL OF THE FRENCH

It is impossible to be certain as to when the Algonquians and Iroquoians first came in contact with men who possessed a secret which could give life to the patience of the former and profit to the activity of the latter — I mean the Christians of Europe. Greenland is not a very great distance from Canada, not farther than New Foundland is from the State of Maine, and for more than two centuries of the Middle Ages, the part of Greenland nearest Canada was a part of Europe. It was inhabited by Norsemen, who were Christians and who had sixteen churches and several monasteries. Greenland existed long enough as a part of Europe to have eighteen bishops appointed to it from Rome, and it was closely enough connected with Europe to send ivory tusks to the Pope as a contribution toward the expense of a crusade. It is recorded that one bishop, Bishop Erik Guapson, in 1121 set out for the lands to the west, that is toward Canada, which had been discovered a hundred years previous. Thus in the days of the Norman Conquest of England, the Norse were near to the Algonquians. Who knows but that they may have visited them ?

In another way the Algonquians may have set their eyes on Europeans. Fishermen from Brittany and from the Bay

of Biscay had long been in the habit of setting out to the
northwest for fishing grounds. No fishermen like to divulge
where they get their best fishing. The English fishermen
fished near Iceland and continued to fish there as their one
regular place of fishing up till the seventeenth century. The
French fishermen, however, were known to be visiting the
Grand Banks of New Foundland so naturally and with so
little sense of innovation immediately after Columbus's voyages to the West Indies, that it has occurred to historians that
they may have been fishing there even before Columbus's land-
fall. If they did so, they too may have come upon Algonquian
Indians on the islands which were so convenient to land on,
and may have been seen by those Indians in the early fifteenth
century when the Europeans were deserting Greenland.

So far as we can see, however, the Algonquians had never
recorded these visits in their traditions. Their legends of
strange men, bright as the sun, who were to arrive from the
East can just as well be derived from messianic myths which
the human heart anywhere can easily coin. Neither did the
Algonquians, from any Europeans whom they may have seen,
learn any Christian doctrines that could afterwards be recognized as Christian. As for the Iroquoians, it is hard to imagine how they could possibly have seen, much less listened
to, a White Man, before the voyages of Columbus.

Within thirty years of Columbus's first voyage, however,
certainly the Algonquians and very likely the Iroquois looked
upon White Men. Various explorers visited the Atlantic coast
of North America : Cabot for the English King, Fernandez,
and then Corte-Real and then Fagundes for the Portuguese,

and finally Verrazano, sailing for the French. Also the fishermen, especially French and Portuguese, visited in great numbers the islands off the fishing banks. But the contacts that the explorers made with the Indians were very temporary and must to the Indians have seemed like a dream. As for the fishermen, the most permanent contact they made with the Indians was the capturing of a half a dozen of them and bringing them to Rouen to be there exhibited with their canoe as a kind of side-show. Neither White Men nor Red Men had learned any secret from the other. So far as spiritual communications were concerned they were still three thousand miles apart. After all, these explorers and fishermen could be seen only by those few Indians who happened to be standing on the shore. There had been no penetration of the Indian country.

In the summer of 1534, a new era began. Jacques Cartier, a sea-captain from St. Malo in Brittany, sailed around the northern shore of the island which lies like a useless stopper in the Gulf of the St. Lawrence River, Anticosti, and looked up that gulf, or, thinking in terms of the points of the compass, looked down that gulf—southwesterly. Like the explorers, his forerunners, who had probably never entered even as far as the St. Lawrence, and like his other predecessors, the fishermen, he was primarily a sea-man with no interest in the land except as something to sail by. For that reason it might have seemed that he, as little as they, would be drawn to penetrate among the Indians. But his case was different, for he had come upon a water-way which would lure anyone who started up it to continue on his way up it, especially if, like Cartier, he was seeking, above all, a road, a northwest passage, to the glories and riches of the East. First the St. Lawrence was a gulf, farther up it was a salt-water river, then it was a fresh-water river. Even then an explorer could not be sure that it was a real river — so huge it was — and he still could believe that he was sailing through islands — the Canada Isles as Canada continued to be called for almost another century. Once an explorer like Cartier had entered the St. Lawrence Gulf he could not, from sheer curiosity, turn back utterly; not until he had voyaged so far up the river as to have definitely penetrated among Indians, both Iroquois and Algonquians, for the St. Lawrence was the road of their world.

Cartier had in fact encountered both Iroquoians and Algonquians even before he entered the St. Lawrence River, for the Algonquians were pretty much everywhere — on Prince Edward Island, for instance, where he had landed — and there were Iroquoians — so the historians have decided it — even on the Gaspé Peninsula, where he made his first landing on the North American mainland. It was they who entertained him when he raised his cross at Gaspé itself. But the attraction of the St. Lawrence brought him ultimately into a much closer contact with both peoples, for in the following year, the year after he had taken his first look southwesterly from Anticosti, he sailed, looking for China, up as far as the rapids above Montreal, which Father Chauchetière described in the letter which begins this book, and which have, ironically enough, themselves been called China, or La Chine. He found on that second voyage Iroquoians (who may have been Mohawks) at Montreal or Hochelaga. He found Iroquoians (who more likely were Hurons) at Quebec. With the latter he wintered.

The wintering gave superficially every prospect of friendship between Red Men and White. When the Algonquians and Iroquoians sighted Cartier and his two ships on his first voyage, which only peered around Anticosti (or as he called it L'Isle de l'Assomption), the Algonquians had generally danced with joy and the Iroquoians had been hospitable. Both these Indian peoples took the Frenchmen for gods. When Cartier arrived on his second voyage with three ships he was similarly welcomed. The fact that he had carried two Indians (Iroquoians) to France with him from Gaspé, without having given them a chance to deliberate as to their willingness to go, had not in the least lessened his prestige. The Iroquoians at Quebec, or Stadacona, had heard of Cartier's first voyage. They were still eager for his friendship.

It is true that there had already been some friction between the Indians and Cartier's men, but it was not due to any fault of the French. The Hurons of Stadacona did not wish to have Cartier go on and up the river to Montreal. To them these ships were a god-send. From the ships they could buy kettles, beads, hatchets. They wished to procure such for their own use, but also in order to resell them to their neighbors. A sense of self-importance, if not of greed, made the Indians at Quebec resent it that Cartier should continue up the river. They told lying tales about the fierceness of those at Hochelaga, and tried to terrify the French through the magic of medicine-men from persisting in wanting to venture westward.

Cartier may have hurt the feelings of the Hurons of Stadacona in leaving them behind, but the reception he received at Hochelaga more than made up for the loss of friendship which the parting had cost him. Once again he was treated as more than human. He was asked to touch the sick and make them well. This put him in a quandary, as he was a humble man. His way out of the difficulty was to act in a very Christian manner. He did not stick his tongue in his cheek, and with a wink of his eye to his companions, proceed to fool the Indians. He wished neither to fool them, nor his God, nor his own self. With a sense of his own unworthiness, and with pity for the Indians, and with a sense of his responsibility as a Christian, he recited over the sick — Christ's sick — the opening of the Gospel of St. John, "In the beginning was the Word" in Latin, which he knew by heart, and then over the same sick he read from one of the Gospels the account of the Passion of Our Lord.

So far Cartier had behaved in a very Christian manner, and as he began his winter with the Hurons at Stadacona he continued to give an example of how Christian a good, honest, ship-captain of St. Malo could be. He told the Indians, through Indian interpreters, of the glories of his religion as he conceived them. He did not rob the Indians. Quite spontaneously he showed his supernatural faith, building in the woods a shrine to Our Lady of Rocamadour, and leading his men in pilgrimage to it, in order to pray for their deliverance from the scurvy which was killing every other man of his crew. Not even in the spring when he captured the chief's son and held him hostage, was he acting rashly or cruelly, or treating the Indians as beings without human rights.

Yet this winter did not cement any friendship between the White Men and the Indians. It so much broke it that Cartier, the next time he camped in Canada, chose a place for his camp as far removed as possible from those who had formerly been his friends. There was no apparent single offense on the part of the French or on the part of the Hurons that had brought this situation to pass. It was simply due to a misunderstanding.

The Indians began by thinking him and his men superhuman ; men of iron they called them. They stood in awe of him and of his religion. When Cartier landed at Gaspé he tried to teach the Iroquoians there something of his Christian belief. Standing in front of the cross which he had raised as the emblem on which to engrave Francis I's claim to the country, he acted a dumb show.

"We all of us," he says, "knelt down, folded our hands in adoration of what was before us, and made signs to the Indians by looking at the sky, and pointing to them to look also at the sky, that in this cross was our salvation."

This converted no Indians, but it gave them to understand that Cartier was in communication with some very powerful spirits, and they were duly impressed. Similarly were the Indians at Stadacona and at Hochelaga impressed at the wonders of the religion of the White Men, which provided them with iron kettles and with ships winged with clouds that could carry whole villages of men.

But then the White Men in the winter began to die. Those that lived lived only because the Indians themselves showed them what herbs to chew in order to be rid of their fever. Far from being helped by their gods, these Frenchmen seemed to worship powerless gods. Their marching to a shrine wherein was depicted the Mother of Him whom they called Christ brought them no evident good. The Indians began by expecting too much of the French. Their disenchantment brought a feeling of revulsion against the Europeans' visions, and a mistrust in their religion.

Cartier on his part tried to understand the Indians. He tried to understand them linguistically, and even during his first brief encounter with the Iroquoians at Gaspé began to make a dictionary of their words. They had a word *isnez,* he said, for the sun, and a word *carnet* for the heavens, but no word, so far as he could learn, for God. Later on he did not despise the Indians of Stadacona because they were poor ; he rather had pity on them. He was glad to learn from them what they knew about herbs, and too ready to believe everything they said about geography, concerning which they usually told him exactly what he wanted to hear. Even when some of the promises of the Indians — as he interpreted them — were proven false, he did not curse the Red Men as liars. He believed that they could easily be turned into Christians.

And yet he did make his mistakes, which were inevitable. He could conceive of the savages only as Europeans who were merely rudimentary Europeans, Breton peasants and

Breton fishermen, who were poorer in worldly goods, and less informed than those of Brittany. When at Hochelaga he came on a long-house filled with young Iroquoian girls he could only explain the use of the house by thinking of it as an abode of viciousness. As a matter of fact, such a resort as he conceived it to be was unknown among the Iroquois, or other American Indians. What he found was, according to Father Lafitau,* the wise Jesuit anthropologist who made his investigations during the first quarter of the eighteenth century, a lodge of vestal virgins. Father Lafitau had the testimony of some of his predecessors that such lodges had existed among the Onondagas until nearly through the seventeenth century, and he had his own observations of the American Indians of the West Indies to consult, not to mention the information which he had gathered concerning the civilizations of Mexico and Peru. He was therefore qualified to make a correct judgment, and probably did. That Cartier with the best intentions in the world should have got things just wrong is significant of the difficulties that he faced.

There was a barrier between the Christian Cartier and his Indians that was not easy to break down. No mere learning of an Indian language could have broken it down, for the culture of the Indians was too different from that of the Europeans to enable them really to understand one another on anything spiritual, on anything less definite than saying "Give me a piece of bread," or "Take this oar." More than goodwill was necessary to break down this barrier : a language

* See Lafitau, *Moeurs des Sauvages Ameriquains*, Paris, 1724, vol. 1, p. 160.

deeper than language, the language of charity itself which could only be spoken by those who really loved the Indians with a love above self-interest. Cartier was kind to the Indians, but he could not love them as one could do who was giving his life for them. Cartier was merely passing them by, or trying to pass them by, in order that for France and for his King, he might find China. As he halted here or there with them, he treated them with much more consideration than he might have, which was something, but not all. When he sailed back to France in 1541 after his third and last voyage to Canada, he left behind him among the Indians scarcely an interest in his Christian secret.

The men who continued the contact that Cartier had begun were even less qualified than he to carry the Faith to the Indians. They were merchants. It would be unfair to say that they cared not at all for God or for France and their King, but they were very much preoccupied with private gain. Many of them were Huguenots, but they were indifferent on matters of religion rather than fanatic. Their god of every day was the god Trade. With a few exceptions they were hostile to the Catholic Church only insofar as it touched their acquisitive practices. The Catholic merchants, their companions, were too often of a similar mind to these Huguenots. They were Catholics, yes, but they did not wish the Church to count too much. The Church's attitude toward usury annoyed them, and disquieted them, pleasant as they found the outward look of Catholic ceremonies. Particularly were the merchants, Catholic and Protestant, impatient at the virility of the Jesuits. They much preferred some dear old "abbé" whom they could hookwink, and be nice to. The Jesuits whom Pascal considered so lax were by the merchants accused of "gehannaing" their consciences.

That merchants should have become interested in the shores which Cartier found poverty-stricken and thought only of passing by, may seem extraordinary. It was extraordinary, for an extraordinary thing happened. A lucrative trade, which the European promoters never foresaw, was forced on them by the Indians. The way in which they forced it on them is both drastic and picturesque. Cartier gives a picture of it. The Algonquian Indians, whom he first came upon, greeted him by divesting themselves of their clothing in order to buy from him a bead or a hatchet. Now the favorite Algonquian clothing was beaver-skin, which they wore with the hair turned in. By so wearing it they rubbed off the longer hairs and prepared a smooth pelt which became in Europe of great value, from Russia to Spain. First the fishermen took the beaver-skins, casually. But soon the merchants heard of the trade, and they prepared not to take them casually. They sent ships across the ocean for nothing else. And the profits they made were enormous,* one hundred percent a year. This could not continue with the competition growing, so there came to be an effort by this or that group to gain a monopoly. The groups were French, and the monopoly they each wished to secure had to come from their French King, who more seriously than Spain or England claimed these

---

* How easy it was even as late as 1605 to buy furs for almost nothing is illustrated by the fact that James Rosier (of whom we have spoken) bought from the Maine Indians "40 good Beaver skins, otter skins and sables" for five shillings. See *English and French Voyages*, p. 371.

Canada Isles. In order to bribe him to give them a monopoly they had to offer to found in his interest a colony in Canada, in order to keep Canada for France.

Such was the game that was played in Canadian history for a hundred years after Cartier's first voyage. The entire story of it would be long to tell, but in order to show what effect these merchant enterprises had on the Indians it is well to tell the story of the founding of Acadia.

In 1604 a colonizing enterprise set out from Havre. At the head of it was De Monts, a Huguenot soldier, who had during the last five years taken to enriching himself in Canada. He was a sturdy enough soldier, who had won the esteem and gratitude of Henry IV. From Henry IV he had been able to win also a monopolistic right to the fur-trade, for which he had to pay by establishing a colony in Canada, and also by converting the Indians. Over a huge tract extending from Philadelphia, along the sea-coast, as far north as Quebec, a region with the name La Cadie (or as we put it Acadia), he was to be by the King's patent, sovereign.

De Monts, like most of the early founders of American colonies, chose the site of his colony somewhat haphazard. He circled around the south hook of Nova Scotia into the Bay of Fundy, and established a settlement on the Island of St. Croix. Before he had even landed he had made his position ticklish by capturing in the Bay of Fundy a Basque vessel which was piled high with furs. The vessel knew nothing of his monopoly, but he made the vessel aware of it, confiscating the furs. De Monts had sense enough to know that all the other traders were jealous of him, and would try to find fault with him. He had to succeed in his colony, or it would be pointed out to the King that he was not keeping his contract. For our purposes it is particularly interesting how he kept one part of the contract, that which related to the conversion of the savages.

The colony of De Monts was very fortunate in finding itself neighbor to a group of unspoiled Algonquians, called Etche-mins. Their sachem Membertu gave such an impression of aged dignity that he was by the French presented with the sum of a hundred years as those of his life. His copper-colored comrades, who were not so much interested in count-ing as the French, referred to his years as numerous as leaves of a tree. Membertu was old and was kind. He helped the French leave their impossible site on the Island of St. Croix, and to establish themselves sanely on the mainland at Port Royal. During the first winter nothing was done towards converting Membertu and his friendly companions. There were two priests with the expedition, but both of them had been chosen it would seem to fulfill a bargain, rather than to be real missionaries. One of them, according to legend, spent his time quarrelling with a Protestant pastor who also accompanied the expedition, and who more than quarrelled back. At any rate both of the priests, and the Huguenot pastor also, died in the first dreadful winter on the Island of St. Croix. During the next three years not a single Indian was converted, nor was any attempt made to convert them. As a result of this and other breaches of contract the monopoly was in 1607 revoked. The colonists sailed back to France.

This did not end the story of the French merchants and

their Indian neighbors in Acadia. A French gentleman, one of the original colonists under De Monts, Poutrincourt, decided to re-establish the colony even without the monopoly. He took therefore the place of De Monts as the lord of Port Royal and sailed in 1610 for the Canada Isles. He had inherited some money from his mother. He had discovered a very rich man, Monsieur Robin, who was willing to invest in the enterprise. Therefore he stepped aboard a well-provisioned ship, and in spite of a mutiny arrived in the early spring at Port Royal. Before him were the buildings of the former settlement, which Membertu, who, if he had formerly been a hundred, was now a hundred and three, was faithfully guarding. Poutrincourt was now the master of the place. He would not make any of the mistakes that the Huguenot De Monts had let himself make.

One of the first things that he set about doing, with the decision of an able promoter, was the conversion of Membertu and of his handful of Algonquian retainers. Poutrincourt was a Catholic, whereas De Monts had been a Protestant, but the zeal of Poutrincourt in converting these savages cannot all be attributed to his Catholicism. Poutrincourt had found it necessary to have the grant of Port Royal, made to him by De Monts, confirmed by the King. The King had confirmed it, but he had commanded that Poutrincourt should carry with him, as missionaries, two Jesuits : Biard and Massé. This vexed very much Poutrincourt, so much indeed that he preferred to take a chance. He left without the Jesuits, counting that he himself could convert the Indians, and thus render the sending of the Jesuits unnecessary. He did take with him a decently obedient priest, the Abbé La Flèche.

Within two months of Poutrincourt's arrival at Port Royal, Membertu with twenty of his followers were solemnly baptized by the amenable Abbé Flèche. Cannons were fired. Membertu had had his name changed. He was no longer Membertu, he was Henri, after Henry of Navarre.

The Abbé La Flèche who did the baptizing was utterly in the dark. He did not know a single Algonquian word, and the Algonquians knew no French. He who had acted as catechist was Biencourt, the ready son of Poutrincourt. He was eighteen years old and ready to help his father. He did know a few words of the Indian tongue (more than he understood of his catechism in French perhaps). As a result the Indians knew not at all what was happening to them. Most of them thought they were being made *Normands* as they called the French in general. Membertu was aware that a youngster had tried to teach him something, but it was nothing — so he later insisted — that he did not know already.

While these "business-men" of the seventeenth century were acting this farce in the New World, a new group in France was beginning to take an interest in the Isles of Canada. They were those people in whom at this time, as if by the passing of a wind, a spiritual spark had been quickened into a flame. They were people whose motive for looking at Canada or New France was not primarily patriotic, and still less commercial : it was apostolic. They wished to convert the savages. They were the embodiment of a great rising religious enthusiasm : the somewhat late counter-reformation in France.

It is impossible to read any kind of a French history without getting some impression of these people whom I have belittlingly called a group, but it is very possible to escape getting a true impression of them. In some histories written by the spiritually blind, they were all of them Tartuffes, hypocrites, like Molière's Tartuffe. To others they were zealots — sincere enough, too sincere — who even disturbed the peace by their impatience. They beat people who did not know what the Blessed Sacrament was, for not showing due respect to it. In other quite different histories they are treated as so many impeccable reflections of the great loving saints of the day, St. Francis de Sales, and St. Vincent de Paul. It is best to think of these people as a motley group, as all Catholic groups are motley. There may have been Tartuffes among them. There surely were people among them who had more zeal than discretion, but just as surely there were saints, hundreds of them, even aside from the canonized saints.

One of the main things to remember about this movement is that it was huge. It was not confined to any class of society, nor to people of any one disposition. It was not a bevy of easily led humanity aroused by priests, or especially by those in religious orders. In many cases the laity took the lead. It was laymen indeed who introduced some of the religious orders, like the reformed Carmelites, into France. It was not an affair of the sacristies, although the teaching of catechism from the sacristies may have helped origin it. It was not a Jesuit scheme, nor a Capuchin scheme, nor the machination of a Cardinal, nor the plan of a Pope. It was huger than that.

Like all Christian movements it out-ran organization. The Company of the Blessed Sacrament, for instance, which sprang up in France at this time, never had any full ecclesiastical approbation. It was a spontaneous affiliation and rising up of people, almost entirely laymen, enthusiastic to accomplish something for Christ. No real religious order was back of it. No individual organizer really ever planned it. The bishops were often embarrassed by it. Yet it spread over France and became so powerful that the royal power in anxiety put an end to it. Many things happened in this movement which were planned for and prayed for. Many wonderful things were accomplished by men who were saints and who have since become familiar to us as people to whom we pray. But how many wonderful things also were accomplished by people who will never be classed as saints, who will never be canonized! Such odd inexpressible men acted in that Christian up-rising — some of them so superficially grotesque. Take Dauversière, for instance, an uncomely, and according to Francis Parkman, vacant-faced tax collector, who dreamed the city of Montreal, Canada, and who founded the city, and who though Parkman called him a fool, and though he seemed to be a fool, was most surely used by God without apologies. The priests were positively embarrassed by the number of Dauversières there were in France at this time, and by the pseudo-Dauversières also.

Another characteristic of this movement which was to dethrone the merchants in New France, and to rule in New France until the coming of age of Louis XIV in 1661, was its unexpectedness. Such unaccountable paradoxes shone in the lives of those who were a part of it. Take the cases of the two saintly women who in succession bore the name of Marie de L'Incarnation : Madame Acarie of Paris and Madame Martin of Tours. Both of them were married women, excellent house-keepers, much abler than their husbands, and possessing in full all the qualities usually referred to as prosaic. Neither of them ever acted inadvisedly or in excitement. Neither of them tried anything practical without bringing it to success. Yet both of them were visionaries in the sense that they were seized from time to time with visions. Their worldly wisdom was not destroyed but it was increased by their ecstatic experiences.

The whole life of Madame Acarie was a series of unexpected events. Certainly her husband never expected what was to happen. He was afraid, to begin with, that she was becoming frivolous, for he found her reading a novel, and he presented her instead with a book of devotion. From that time on, what went on in his wife's soul was beyond his ken. Sometimes, as the years went on, at the mere mention of the name of Our Lord, she would swoon. She became the mystic among mystics. She brought the Carmelites of Saint Theresa of Avila to Paris. Her influence was so great in Paris that religion became a thing of fashion. Young ladies wore veils in the streets, in order to appear like Carmelites. Her counsel helped fill the Benedictine and Visitation convents with novices.

And yet while she played this part, she continued to be Madame Acarie, to care for her Quixotic but helpless husband, to manage his affairs, and even extricate him from legal difficulties. While it was her followers who began to wear veils in the streets as if they were nuns, it was she who rebuked them for so doing. There was nothing of a falsely exalted person about her. Although she encouraged some young girls to become nuns, the number she encouraged was nothing in comparison with the number she discouraged. As for herself, she did not become a nun until her husband had been buried, and her children provided for. Then she became a Carmelite quite without precipitation.

Madame Acarie was very typical of her age, and of the way its spirituality showed itself, and so was the second Marie de L'Incarnation, Marie Guyard, who married a Monsieur Martin. She was never called on to be the lawyer like Madame Acarie, and she did not have to spend a large part of her life taking care of a foolish husband — for her husband died after two years of married life, when she was just twenty — but she was a marvelous administrator. She managed a Transportation Company by which her family lived when there was no one left in the family to manage it. But even while she was conducting her family's affairs competently like a man, she began to be attacked by visions. Like Madame Acarie she underwent many trances. They were not of her choosing, but she accepted them. Similarly, as in the case of the first Marie, these experiences seemed to complete her strength, and to give roundness to her character. When they dragged her by their impulsion into an Ursuline Monastery it seemed for a time that they were leading her to abandon some of her abilities, but not so. As an Ursuline she was sent to Quebec there to found a house of her order where there

were only a score of houses of any kind at all, and where
the difficulties of living demanded the greatest resourcefulness.
In the case of Marie de L'Incarnation, as in the case of Madame
Acarie, and as in the case of many lesser figures in this period
in France, it seemed as if God — if you will pardon the apparent irreverence in the phrase — acted with unwonted and
glorious abruptness.

So while the traders were dallying with the souls of Indians
in New France, a sudden missionary enthusiasm was rising
in France out of this spiritual revival, and one person actuated
by that enthusiasm suddenly entered into unexpected relations
with Nova Scotia. The person was a lady, Antoinette de
Pons, Marquise de Guercheville. She was a woman of family
— her uncle being the future Cardinal de Richelieu ; she was a
woman of honor, having repulsed the wooings of Henry IV ;
and she was a spiritual woman by a real and growing Christian zeal. When Poutrincourt had sailed for Canada in 1610
without the Jesuits she had been indignant. In 1611 Biencourt arrived back in Paris with an account of his baptisms,
but she was still indignant. Henry IV had recently been
assassinated. He could not order the Jesuits to Nova Scotia,
but Marie de' Medici, his wife, actuated by the Marquise de
Guercheville, could and did. This put Biencourt in a real
difficulty. To begin with, he did not himself want the Jesuits. Secondly his backers who were Huguenot capital-
ists refused to supply the funds for a return voyage if Jesuits
were to ride on their vessel. At this moment the Marquise
de Guercheville lost her patience. She herself bought the

vessel and supplied the funds, and sent the surprised Biencourt and the surprised Jesuits across the ocean.

It was royally done. Truly her act was like a breath of fresh air in this dilly-dallying of calculating merchants. But it was not wholly wise. It increased the anger of the Huguenot traders and of all the traders against the Jesuits. It put the Jesuits themselves in an awkward position. They crossed the sea not as humble missionaries, but as proprietors, for she made them her agents.

Like rash and royal acts it accomplished some very great immediate good. It was a very great thing to have Fathers Massé and Biard arrive in Nova Scotia at all. Biard was a writer and scholar, Massé was of a different type, simpler, whose utility, humble and indispensable, earned him the title Père Utile (Father Useful). Both of them set to work to learn the Algonquian tongue, and Father Massé befriended the Indians by actually passing the winter with them. Father Biard made a real Christian out of Membertu. He instructed him for the baptism he had already received, heard his confession on the Indian's death-bed, and at the old chieftain's request saw that he received a Christian burial. Old Membertu had been one of the rare Algonquian sachems who had but one wife. That made his true conversion easier. With some of the other Indians it was more difficult. They had been baptized by Abbé La Flèche without being informed that eight wives were too many. Both the Jesuits accomplished much, and in that much should be included the writing of letters home which excited a great interest in Canada among those who were animated by the contemporary religious revival, and which initiated the series of Jesuit Relations from New France.

And yet this good was being accomplished at a great cost : at the cost of a growing ineradicable enmity between the traders and the Jesuits. The Marquise de Guercheville, in making the Jesuits her agents, had set them up as competitors to Poutrincourt and the Protestants. That they had no purpose of trading made no difference. They were treated as rivals with whom to quarrel, and on whom all unsuccess could be blamed. Inasmuch as there was plenty of unsuccess, there was plenty to blame on them, and the colonists, who had the mood of those who had expected great things and received nothing, were quite ready to believe any story of any Jesuit in order to be able to explain their miscalculations. Calumnies that had spread from France, and that were nourished by the grievances of the colonists, ended by making the Jesuits an object of general suspicion : they were robbing Port Royal, they were starving it. This brought a kind of daily persecution on Fathers Massé and Biard, which might have been tolerable, except that the persecution took the vindictive method of trying to frustrate their missionary efforts.

When things had grown so bad that the Marquise de Guercheville was aware of the impossible situation the Jesuits were in, she made another royal move. She sent out her own colonization expedition, which stopped at Port Royal, took aboard the two Jesuits, and then proceeded to settle on the Island of Mount Desert in what is now the United States. So far she had manoeuvered well. She had received grants from De Monts which Poutrincourt did not know De Monts could still give. Possibly something might have come of her colony, if a month after its arrival an English ship commanded by a captain who can scarcely be thought of as other than a pirate, Argall, descended upon it, sent fifteen men of it adrift in an open boat and carried the rest of them back to England. In his same raid he had destroyed the settlement at Port Royal. Thus the entire Acadian enterprise ended in futility. Although a few Indians had been converted, some of whom clung to the Faith, and were discovered later here and there — one woman as far away as Tadoussac at the confluence of the St. Lawrence and Saguenay — yet the respect of the Algonquians for Europeans and for the Christian Faith which they hid or expressed had not increased. Father Biard was surprised that the Algonquians continued to consider themselves as superior to the French. Considering the comedy that the French had played, his surprise was scarcely justified.

After the temporary ending of Acadia, a somewhat similar drama to the Acadian one was played on the St. Lawrence at Quebec, which drama had a similar end, but fraught with much happier consequences. It was due to the loss by De Monts of his first monopoly that Quebec was founded at all. In 1607, when De Monts could no longer look to Port Royal, he began to regard the St. Lawrence River, which he had already visited. In 1608 he sent the navigator, Champlain, who had once helped him to found Port Royal, to a rounded hill called Kebec which looked like a natural fort, on the north bank of the St. Lawrence where the river turns from a gulf into a river, there to establish a trading-post. De Monts this time was less interested than at Port Royal in establishing a colony, but he did need a fort, against rival traders of his own nation and those of others.

It was so much a mere trading-post, and a Huguenot one at that, that the pious Catholics of France, who were interested in missionary ventures, decided not to pay much attention to it. The Marquise de Guercheville did not plead its cause at Court. The Jesuits who were invited to sail to Quebec, declined.

But circumstances changed. Once again a monopolistic company was formed, which had its contract to keep with the new King Louis XIII. This connected the trading-post at Quebec, which was the trading-post of the new company, with the royal government, and not so exclusively with the traders. Then for a second time, in 1614, owing to Argall, Port Royal came to an end. There was only one place in Canada now, one obvious place where missionary activity could be carried on. Quebec began to be looked on by the Marquise de Guercheville and her friends with a different eye.

Still another thing recommended Quebec as a possible seat of missionary enterprise: Champlain was the governor there. He was a Catholic, and not merely an apathetic Catholic; he had been touched by the spiritual revival in France. He was genuinely religious, and so incapable of mercenary transactions that he was quite unfitted to be a trader. He was an explorer, a geographer, a soldier, but a wretched merchant. Thus it was he who gave a spiritual turn to the new trading-post. Since the Jesuits had not wished to join De

Monts, he inquired of a friend of his, a fellow-citizen of his native city, Brouage, Sieur Houel, Controller-General of the Salt Works, a man even more identified with the religious revival than he, as to what priests would come to Canada. Sieur Houel recommended the Recollets (who were Franciscans), so Champlain invited the Recollets, raising for their transportation and support by his own efforts from private sources 1500 livres.* The Recollets arrived in Canada at Quebec in June, 1615.

This did not very much bother the traders. The Franciscans were but three in number — two priests, one lay brother — and though they were very enterprising and went as far as Lake Huron, there to live among the most northern Iroquians, and though they also set up a neat convent at Quebec where wheat and vegetables were grown, they really did not count. They had not money enough to establish anything like a Reduction for the wandering Indians. What good influence they may have had among the Hurons near Lake Huron was nullified by the influence of the law-free trappers who outnumbered them six to one. They did make friends with the Indians, who grew to like them, but they could not protect the Indians from the rapacities of commerce. Liquor was becoming the most effective thing with which the White Men could buy furs cheap. The traders smiled kindly enough at the Recollets, knowing they were helpless. Their friend Champlain was busy in explorations, which were his chief interest.

But if the traders were satisfied with the Recollets, the Re-

* *Voyages of Samuel de Champlain*, New York, 1907, p. 277.

collets were not satisfied with the traders. They began by giving to the traders advice. They tried to persuade the company to found a colony, a real agricultural one, at Quebec. The traders did not take the advice—as late as 1620 there were only two permanent French families at Quebec. Neither did they wish to take the advice. Agriculture would spoil the fur-trade. A large conspicuous colony would bring the Dutch, or the English or the Spanish upon them. They wished to escape notice.

Finally the Recollets, feeling that they must have help, invited the Jesuits to join them. They believed that the Jesuits could help them with their numbers, there being at this time fifteen hundred Jesuits in France, and that they could help them with influence at the Court. But the Jesuits —three of them priests, Fathers Massé, de Brébeuf, and Charles Lalemant, and two of them lay brothers—found, when they arrived in 1625 in Canada, that they were as helpless as the Recollets. The traders wished to shackle them in their attempts to make the Indians anything but victims of European commerce.

But the battle was now on, for the Jesuits did try to do what they could do at Court, and the Marquise de Guercheville began to take an interest in Quebec. Finally she led her uncle, Cardinal Richelieu, to take an interest. He wished France to have colonies, and it was certain that the company colonizing Quebec was not colonizing it. Therefore it was not due to sentimentalism that he moved. Nor need it be claimed that he moved from purely spiritual motives. As a guarder of the interests of France, he had a right to be dissatisfied with the traders. Therefore he stepped in, somewhat after the manner of his niece. He formed a new company, put himself at its head, threw out the Huguenot promoters.

The new company which he formed received its charter in April, 1627. It was called the "Company of New France" or "The Company of the Hundred Associates." Those who made up the hundred were not all of them primarily interested in missionary enterprises, any more than was Richelieu himself, but they were not out for private gain. The majority of them were state officials,* officers connected with the finances of France. Among these officials was our friend Louis Houel, of Brouage, who was as pious as he was skilful in money affairs, and he no doubt was but one of many similar officials who were both officials and pious. There were nobles among them, there were bourgeois, but not more than twenty who were classed as merchants.

Of these associates Cardinal Richelieu demanded one thing above all, that they "make every effort to people New France or Canada." Before fifteen years were up they were bound to have two thousand colonists on the other side of the Atlantic. They were to transport them free, and to support them for three years. In order to be able to do this the associates had to subscribe three hundred thousand livres, to be paid in three annual instalments. To reimburse them for this very great expense, they were to receive the monopolistic rights for fifteen years in the fur-trade, and for themselves and their heirs, in perpetuity, rights that were practically sovereign to an extent of territory vaguely confined between Florida and the

* See E. Salone, *La Colonisation de la Nouvelle France*, Paris, p. 40.

Arctic Circle. After fifteen years were up they would not have to transport and support any more colonists, not at their own expense.

The new company thus created by Richelieu put an end, on paper at least, to the reign of the merchants and the Huguenots, but in reality no great change was effected on the American side of the ocean. Many officers of the trading fleet and agents of the company were Huguenots and continued to hold the situation in their hands. They were in a position to snap their fingers at the Associates in France. Nevertheless, the power might ultimately have been wrested from them simply by the action of the Associates themselves. In the spring of 1629 the latter sent across the ocean two vessels containing over two hundred colonists. Such a number of farmers and artisans would have completely changed the aspect and character of Quebec, had they arrived. But they never arrived.

They did not arrive, because in 1628 Charles I of England had declared war on France in order to help the French Huguenots at La Rochelle, and an English fleet intercepted them in the summer of 1629 as they arrived at the mouth of the St. Lawrence River. The same fleet captured Quebec from Champlain and sent him in honor but in chagrin back to his fatherland. A few French traders and one French family, the Héberts, remained at Quebec, but the flag above the fort there was now an English flag.

This turn of events, which must have seemed to Champlain a terrible disaster, really accomplished what the Hundred Associates might not have been able to accomplish themselves.

It cleared Canada of the merchants and the merely merchant spirit. It is a mistake to think of this capture as an act of international warfare, or even as warfare between Catholics and Protestants. It is true that the fleet which made the capture was more a Huguenot fleet than an English one, at least in its leadership, but many of the French sailors and captains against whom they fought were also Huguenots. Truly the capture was but an unedifying quarrel between merchants. Kirk, the English commander, was half French, and married to a French wife. He was by the French considered as a citizen of Dieppe, where he lived. In capturing Quebec he was capturing for himself and his friends the fur-trade. In ousting Champlain he ousted with him the last traces of the particular Huguenot and merchant influence of which Richelieu had tried to get rid. He had cleaned the slate as only a rival merchant could, leaving it to the French in their turn to oust him.

CHAPTER V

THE MISSIONARY EFFORT

IN 1632 the French did oust him. Even before Kirk (or Kertk as the French liked to call him, as if he were an out and out Breton) had captured Quebec, peace had been made between France and England, as Kirk was aware even at the time. So the restoration of Canada to France was only a matter of common justice. Even then the restoration might not have been insisted on by France if Richelieu had not set his heart on creating New France in Canada. It was he who saw to it that the treaty of St. Germain in 1632 confirmed the restoration. It was he who sent over a fleet to take possession of Quebec. And the fleet was strong enough on its arrival to enforce the ousting.

The slate was now literally washed clean. The very trading-post had almost disappeared. The roof of the store-house was falling in. The chapel which had been used as a store-house had lost its door. Only one building besides the fort seemed still alive, and that was the house of Widow Hébert who had clung to the soil like a true colonist. Into her house hastened the two Jesuit priests, who had accompanied the French fleet ; and, as a re-beginning of New France, they there celebrated their first Mass.

With this Mass began an era which was to last for over

thirty years, during which the most Christian element in France was to dominate in New France. The destiny of a land which had once been in the hands of mere traders was to lie for well over a generation in the hands of that portion of the French people — that large portion — who were some of them saints, and all of them fervent, who were some of them able and others of them inept, but who were all of them animated by a noble intention, which gave a distinction and generosity to all that they touched. The chance which the Marquise de Guercheville had been more than praying for had arrived.

These spiritual, other-worldly people could never have kept control over Canada during these years if they had not possessed the sovereign powers conferred on them — or on their representatives the Company of the Hundred Associates — by Cardinal Richelieu, and they were canny enough to preserve them, even though it was not easy. When in 1633 they found themselves without funds, they sold their trading rights for five years to a subsidiary company for 10,000 livres. It was, I suspect, a bargain in which they came off second best, yet in it they did not relinquish their control of the traders, and of New France as a whole. It was, I say, all-important that they should guard these privileges, in order to remain dominant ; but even with these privileges they might have played a secondary part, if circumstances had not favored them, and if they had not acted with great energy.

The circumstances that favored them were circumstances that also handicapped them. They were these : The French King, Louis XIII, and his masterful minister, Cardinal Richelieu, were too occupied with the internal reorganization of France, and with France's war in Germany, to take the interest they might otherwise have taken in New France. Cardinal Richelieu had a very much more nationalistic plan in New France than had the spiritual people whose deeds I am to celebrate. That he did not enforce his plan, and set aside one which had less earthly ambitions than his, was due only to circumstances over which the spiritual people had no control. It was a piece of good fortune for them in that it freed their hands, but also a great hardship. The active help of Richelieu would have made their exploits less lasting, less lovable, but much more spectacular.

In Canada itself the pious people were thus allowed to help themselves, without arms, without soldiers, without any hoard of treasure at their disposal; and help themselves they did. Instead of letting those marvellously courageous trappers, the *coureurs de bois,* turn all of Canada into their private reserve, instead of letting the merchants — those few of them among the Hundred Associates, and those others who had bought the trading rights — direct the planting of the settlements, they themselves in the person of missionaries, who were laymen as well as priests, went farther into the forests than the trappers, and were more energetic than those who sought profits, in establishing colonies, and building forts. The great men of action, the heroes of New France from 1633 to 1663 were all not merely Christians; they were thorough and admirable Christians.

Champlain, who was one of these thorough Christians, arrived back in New France in 1633, to take up the duties of

Governor of the country. He was now, not only in fact and in title, governor, but he found himself unhampered by the greedy merchants who had formerly worked secretly and openly against him. He began to rule at Quebec in a very Christian way. He had his little fort on the hill, and his chapel near it : Notre Dame de la Recouvrance, which he had built in gratitude for the recovery of his dearly beloved citadel. At his table sat the Admiral du Plessis, as stalwart a Christian as he was, and de Lauzon, the Intendant, who, as the Jesuits said, was "affectionate to all their projects." These officials at the fort ruled their lives in a semi-monastic way. At their mid-day meal they listened to reading concerning the famous heroes of old. At their evening meal they listened to lives of the saints. They prayed with the Angelus. They lived by the Angelus. Around them were gathering a slowly growing community of colonists, who took ten years to number two hundred, but who, though few, had been chosen for their piety and integrity, and who showed themselves hardy and righteous. They made of the entire village of Quebec a mission.

But there were also professional missionaries at the mission : the Jesuits. Five of them crossed the ocean to Canada in 1632, of which five, Father Le Jeune, Father Anne de Noue, (a converted courtier), and a lay-brother, landed at Quebec, the others halting at Cape Breton Island. The next year another group arrived, among whom was Father de Brébeuf who had already spent three years in the country. The next year an equally famous Jesuit, Father Jogues, arrived. Before eight years passed by, there were seventeen Jesuit priests in New France. They inherited the old task that they and the Recollets had previously faced together, and they analyzed its difficulties much as the Recollets had analyzed them.

Their great opportunity they considered to be that with the Hurons on Georgian Bay, those northernmost Iroqouians, whom the Iroquois would never forgive for not having joined the League. The Hurons were difficult of access, for it took at least thirty days to arrive at them from Quebec. Nine hundred miles had to be paddled and tramped, first two hundred miles up the St. Lawrence, then up the Ottawa River, then across Lake Nipissing, then down French River to Lake Huron, then down the shores of Lake Huron to where is now Midland, Ontario. But this very remoteness was an advantage, for it gave the missionaries a chance to keep the Indians segregated from some of the demoralizing influences brought in by the traders and trappers — brandy for instance. But most important of all, the Hurons were sedentary. They lived, twenty thousand of them, in populous villages in an area little over thirty miles by thirty miles square. They were not always vanishing away. They could be kept track of.

Set beside this opportunity was the other less inviting opportunity : that with the wandering tribes, the Algonquians. These latter were here and there and everywhere, but never many in the same place. The poorest of them, according to the Recollet historian Sagard,* were the Montagnais tribe which wandered in a region a hundred miles toward the sea

* F. Gabriel Sagard-Theodat crossed to New France in 1624, and wrote Le Grand Voyage au Pays de Hurons, Paris, 1632.

from Quebec, on the northern bank of the St. Lawrence near Tadoussac. The richest of these Algonquian tribes was the Algonquin tribe itself, which roamed on the northern bank of the St. Lawrence, a hundred miles above Quebec. These Algonquian tribes, especially the Montagnais, had been in contact with the European traders for almost a century. They had learned so well from the traders how to drive hard bargains, that now the traders were using brandy to outwit them. This made their evangelization difficult. And another thing that made it difficult was their habit of wandering here and there in small groups. A man who had become half-instructed, and who showed great promise, might never be seen again.

Father Paul Le Jeune, who had been brought up a Huguenot, and had then become a Catholic, then a Jesuit, and as a Jesuit had held office as rector of a college at Dieppe, was officially responsible for taking advantage of both these opportunities : the good one, and the less good one. But really it was impossible for anyone at Quebec to direct the missionary activity among the Hurons. Only once a year did letters pass between the two places. Therefore the two opportunities had to be considered by him, as they will have to be now considered by us, as two separate affairs. He entrusted the evangelization of Huronia to Father de Brébeuf. He himself took charge of the less interesting but nearer opportunity, that among the Algonquians.

The first thing he did had been done before by his predecessors, even by de Brébeuf, but it still remained the right thing to do. He made himself a school-boy, went among the

Montagnais to learn from the Montagnais. "So I embarked in their shallop," he says, "on the 18th of October (the year was 1633) making profession as a little pupil on precisely the same day that I had previously began the profession of master of our schools." * He joined a winter hunting expedition, with men, women and children, and stayed on it, and lived on it, and nearly died on it — for six months.

On this excursion he learned many things which most heads of colleges do not learn. He learned how to patch his cassock with eel-skins, and how to tear those same eel-skins out of his cassock and dine off them when he was starving. He learned how it feels to be threatened by a medicine-man, "he hissed like a serpent — did the medicine-man — he howled like wolf or like a dog, he screeched like an owl or a night hawk — rolling his eyes about in his head and striking a thousand attitudes always seeming to be looking for something to throw." Le Jeune learned how not to be too much impressed by this spiritualist who pretended he had gone into a trance of madness. "Having touched his pulse and forehead, I found him as cool as a fish, and as far from fever as I was from France. The sorcerer was all method and no madness." †

Father Le Jeune learned good things and bad things about the Montagnais. He was made aware on the first day of his expedition that no one but a fool would have done what he did : bring a small keg of wine with him. One of the Indians who had begged him to bring it, and had promised

* Thaites, vol. VII, p. 71.
† Thwaites, vol. vii, p. 120.

never to take more than was doled out to him, swallowed the whole keg, and became so violent that his comrades could quiet him by no means other than that of dashing a kettle of boiling water full in his face. He learned how handy it is to have an expert hunter as one's friend. Mestigoit was this hunter. He was not a Christian, but he called Father Le Jeune "Nikanis" or Loved One, and at the end of the whole excursion he saved his loved one's life, extending down his foot over an icy precipice so that Father Le Jeune, capsizing in a canoe, could come to dry land. Mestigoit was worth knowing. It was he who explained to Father Le Jeune that it was a part of the Algonquian code to give thanks even when things went wrong.

Another thing that he learned was the Montagnais dialect of the Algonquian tongue. This in itself justified his expedition. By making himself familiar with the language, he not only became able to transact affairs with the Indians directly, instead of through a usually tricky interpreter, and that of being able to translate his prayers into their tongue — "Noukhimane missi ca Khichitaen" (My Captain, all who has made) — but he also discovered how different from his modes were the Algonquian modes of thought. He discovered that all the words which were familiar and over-dear to him as a school-teacher and as a European thinker could not possibly be translated in any direct fashion into Algonquian. Theologians, philosophers, mathematicians, physicians would be at a total loss to find synonyms for their favorite phrases; but the Algonquians, on the other hand, had their own treasure of words which was untranslatable into French. They had an immense number of proper nouns. Their verbs expressed many shadows of meaning, with which our sensibilities do not concern themselves. For instance, the word *to eat,* if *eat* were used absolutely, was *nimitisan,* but if what one ate was mentioned an entirely different verb had to be used. He learned a great deal of humility while he tried to learn the Algonquian language.

Finally he learned something which was of very immediate bearing on his future policy; namely, that the Algonquians were always on the verge of starvation. It was the need of food, so often desperate, that gave the charlatan medicine-men their power, for they claimed that they could provide good luck in hunting. It was lack of food which caused the Montagnais to abandon their sick, as he himself had seen them do, and to kill their aged, as he had heard. Therefore he came to the conclusion that he could lure the wandering tribes to him by offering them food, and by offering to care for their sick and their aged. He was perfectly well aware that this was a form of bribery. He very much doubted if the Algonquians (and here of course he was wrong) were spiritual enough to be affected by the charity which went with the material gift. But it was the only method that was possible of coming in contact with the wanderers. Quite obviously there were not enough Jesuits in New France or Old France to become private chaplains to each hunting party. And he doubted if one in ten could stand the hardships of such a life. The Indians had to be made to come to him. Possibly in the end they could be made to settle down near him.

If Father Le Jeune had had to work alone, or even alone

with his fellow-Jesuits, in putting this scheme into effect, he
would have succeeded in no part of it. Not even in the
material part. It cost something, though not much, to supply
a bowl of hominy to the famished Indians, who soon, in accordance with his wishes, began to call at his mission of Notre
Dame des Anges on the St. Charles River near Quebec, and at
the other mission which he immediately established one
hundred miles up the St. Lawrence at Three Rivers : Notre
Dame de La Conception. A much larger sum was needed
as soon as the Indians, following the same wish of Father Le
Jeune, suggested that they would like to settle down near the
mission, and become sedentary. Fields and houses had to
be supplied for them.

For such needs, however, Father Le Jeune had the backing
of that great number of people in France who at this time
resolved to have Christ's name mean something on this earth.
A trickle of treasure was always arriving from this or that
group of them. In great emergencies a sum would arrive
with an unexpectedness that had grandeur. It was a magnificent diplomat, grown not only pious, but magnificently
pious, who supplied Father Le Jeune with the money to establish an Algonquian settlement at Sillery, six miles up the
St. Lawrence from Quebec. His name was Sillery — Noël
Brulard de Sillery. He had at one time been French Ambassador in Spain and then in Italy, and in those offices had particularly delighted in astonishing himself and others by show
of earthly splendor : by costly furniture, banquet-covered
tables and by a numerous retinue. In 1625 he had transferred
his thoughts from earthly splendors to heavenly ones, and he

turned for advice to St. Vincent de Paul. From then on, he put his money to new uses. He had bought his share in the trading company — that of the Hundred Associates — which had its privileges at Quebec. He made the investment in order to keep Canada in the hands of those who were propitious to the missionaries, and who would not think only of profits. It was a manner of ridding himself of his money. And now he rid himself of still more by presenting to Father Le Jeune a sum sufficient to build a chapel and various mission buildings, and with the help of twenty laborers, to prepare fields that could support the Indians by agriculture. His purpose was to aid the Jesuits in New France "to gather into some convenient place the wandering and vagabond savages, and thus provide a powerful means to their conversion." *

But help of the most tender human devotion was even more necessary than money, in order that after having drawn the savages to him he could have a spiritual effect on them. His greatest help in this respect came from the nuns. This was a time when there was a great increase not only in the number of religious sisters in France, but in the number of true vocations to the various sisterhoods. Many Benedictine convents for women (as well as men) were founded, but still more were re-formed. This good health in spiritual affairs showed also in the founding of various new orders of women. Of these, the three that concern us most are : First, the Reformed Carmelites,† who did the praying, and who must always be

---

* Rochemonteix, *Les Jesuits et La Nouvelle-France*, vol. I, p. 247.

† Le Jeune writes of them: "All this holy order takes arms for us with so much ardor that I am overwhelmed therewith." Thwaites, vol. XI, p. 57.

thought of as all-important in the background of European history at this period. Secondly there were the Hospital Sisters, who were not a complete innovation, but rather a revival of a mediaeval order, which had decayed during the evil days when most of the city hospitals in Europe, even in Catholic Europe, had been either secularized, with a consequent demoralization setting in, or had been disendowed, which brought the consequence of their moneys going inevitably into the hands of those who complained most of the riches of the church — I mean the rich. During the last half century a hundred or more city hospitals, run by religious, had been founded in France. The women who founded them, living in an age which did not call itself feminist, were marvelous examples for feminists to admire. Most of them have been forgotten on this earth. Henri Bremond, in his *Histoire Littéraire du Sentiment Religeux en France,* has revived the memory of a few of them. There was a Suzanne Dubois, for instance, who organized a congregation of nurses, the Hospitallers of Loche, for whom and with whom she founded and maintained seventeen city hospitals in France. Thirdly, there were the Ursulines who had been founded a hundred years before this by an orphan girl on Lake Como, Saint Angela Merici, who had perceived that all girls about her were being orphaned by receiving nothing but a pagan education, and who wished to have them educated as Christians, according to their baptism. During her life Angela had merely presided over a small group of a dozen sublime schoolmistresses. Within twenty-five years after her death, however, her Ursulines had spread over France, Germany and

Italy. Particularly they found fertile soil in France, where during a half century 320 Ursuline houses were established.

Of these three orders, the Carmelites did not cross to Canada. They merely prayed for Canada. Both the Hospitallers and the Ursulines, however, crossed the ocean in 1639, living while on ship-board their life in choir together, like a single order. It is significant how each of these orders came to cross the ocean. It is more or less natural that the Hospitallers should have gone to Canada. They were indeed invited to go there by Father Le Jeune. He had put the idea into the heads of the Hospitallers of Dieppe. The Marquise de Guercheville had raised the funds for them. The only thing extraordinary about their going was their eagerness to go. When the Superior of the Hospital Sisters of Dieppe asked for volunteers to go to Quebec, every sister in Dieppe volunteered. Each had been praying secretly for the opportunity. Such was the interest of spiritual France in New France. The crossing of the Ursulines was, however, less to be expected. Divine prompting had to intervene in a manner more than royal in order to bring the Ursulines to Quebec.

The story runs thus: Marie de L'Incarnation, an Ursuline at Tours, who had run an "express company" before she entered the convent, but had never even heard of Canada, had to see a vision of Our Lady pointing out to her a path towards the rock of Quebec, and Madame de La Peltrie, who knew all about Canada and who wished to send Ursulines there, but who had no way of finding a fitting Ursuline to lead them in such a wilderness, had by impossible coincidence, to be brought face to face with Marie de L'Incarnation, before these

two working together could bring the crossing of the ocean of
the Ursulines to pass. It was all wonderfully complicated but
absolutely simple.

On the first of August 1639, the ship carrying the Ursulines
and the Hospital Sisters, three from each order, arrived at
Quebec. It was a wonderful day for the sisters : they had
been for three months, since May 4th, packed into a ship a
little larger than a whale. It was the day after a great day,
for the day previous had been the feast of St. Ignatius, a feast
very propitious for one arriving in New France ; and the
evening of that day had been pure romance. They had arrived so near to Quebec that they could almost see it. They
had landed on the Isle d'Orleans and slept on the firm land
with nothing between them and the stars, save a few boughs.
They were like the Indians of whom they had read.

And a wonderful day it was too for the city, the city of
two hundred, Quebec. The governor, who was now Montmagny — Champlain being dead — put on all his finery, and
commanded a score of soldiers to march after him, like an
army, and ordered cannon to boom. And behold, the Jesuits
too, marshalled themselves on the shore, a half dozen of them,
Le Jeune in their midst. He was no longer officially their
head, for he had been succeeded by Vimont, but to the colonists, and to the Indians, especially, he was still the chief figure,
and the plan in which they lived was his plan. The coming
of the nurses was a part of his plan. For a moment, just for
a moment, it was all very romantic for Montmagny, for
Le Jeune, for Vimont, for all the colonists. Plans seemed to
be coming true. And it touched their hearts to see such a

dear familiar part of France thus crossing the ocean to them.

But the next day the romance was of another sort. There was a small-pox epidemic at Quebec. There were sick Frenchmen, but mostly the town was flooded with sick Indians. Le Jeune who had wished to attract the Indians had attracted them now for sure. He had himself turned nurse : he and his colleagues. And no sooner had the Hospitallers and Ursulines landed, than they were, all of them, nurses — Ursulines as well as their companions. It was the hot season ; the season of flies and mosquitoes. There was no hospital building, though the Marquise de Guercheville was building one for the sisters from Dieppe at Sillery. There was no neat convent for the Ursulines. In the most inadequate quarters, without sufficient medical supplies, without bedding for the sick, these women from France had to inure themselves to a stench quite different from that of the French hospitals. All during the summer they nursed the sick, for the epidemic lasted till cold weather. There was much labor, little sleep, and there were no pleasant cheerful things like cleanliness or neatness around them, to remind them of their home-land. The comment of Marie de L'Incarnation on this hardship was as usual straight to the point : "All of this was a delight to us more sweet than you can imagine." *

But no matter what the Jesuits may have done to bring some conception of the Christian Faith to the Indians, and no matter what the nuns may have done, all that they did could have been undone by the colonists if they themselves had not behaved like Christians. It was their good morals

* Marie de L'Incarnation, *Ecrits Spirituels* (ed. Jamet), vol. II, p. 272.

which made the vicinity of Quebec a salutary place for the Indians to visit. They lived like Christians and worshipped like Christians. Even the austerest Puritan could not have found fault with their conduct.

But these colonists were more than Puritans : they had a real charity for the Indians. Little details mentioned inadvertently in the Jesuit Relations attest to this. It may be remembered that Father Le Jeune on his winter hunt had been tormented by a medicine-man. Later on, the son of that medicine-man, left an orphan, fell sick of a filthy scrofulous disease. In telling of the child's malady the Jesuit Relations * mention quite casually that Monsieur Gand tended the boy's wounds. Now Monsieur Gand was high enough in the colony to be Commissary General, and rich enough to be one of the Hundred Associates. That he was also humble and charitable enough to care for the son of a particular Indian speaks very well for him. If this story had been told as having to do with Monsieur Gand it might be looked upon as having been related because, like most things in chronicles, it was exceptional, but it was not related primarily of him, but of the Indian boy. And the fact that his action was taken so readily for granted by the Jesuits tempts us to believe that there were others of the colonists who did not think it strange to act in a friendly manner to a people very possibly repugnant to them.

But leaving this aside, it is quite certain that all the French colonists treated the Indians quite regularly as if they were human beings like themselves : a courtesy often more appre-

* See Thwaites, vol. VII, p. 303.

ciated by the recipient than is mere grim justice. The Indians
were allowed to worship in the same chapels, and take part
in the same celebrations with the French. Shortly after the
nuns had arrived there was a civic procession in honor of
the birth of the Dauphin (the future Louis XIV). It took
place on the Feast of the Assumption, and the Indians were
participants not only in the religious but in the national ceremony, which is described as follows in the Relations :

"The day dedicated to the glorious and triumphant Assumption of the blessed Virgin was chosen. At early morn, our
Christian Neophytes came to hear holy Mass, to confess and
to receive communion. All the other savages who were then
in the neighborhood of Kebec assembled, and we placed them
in the order they were to observe. When the procession com-
menced its march the Cross and the banner were carried in
front. Monsieur Gand came next, walking at the head of the
Savage men, the first six of whom were clad in these royal
garments (namely those which had been presented them by
Louis XIII). They went, two by two, most sedately, with
becoming modesty. After the men walked the foundress of
the Ursulines, having beside her three or four Savage girls,
clothed in the French fashion ; then followed all the daughters and wives of the Savages in their own costume, keeping
their ranks perfectly. The Clergy came next ; and after them
walked monsieur our Governor, and our Frenchmen, then
our French women, without any other order than that suggested by humility." *

The surest testimony of all, however, to the good influence

* Thwaites, vol. xv, p. 225.

or the colonists on the Indians lies in the wish of Le Jeune, often expressed, that there were more colonists. He did not plan with those more colonists to drown the Indians in the numbers of the French. He did not expect to turn the Indians through their influence, as Cardinal Richelieu wished him to do, into Frenchmen. But he believed that more colonists like those already in New France could be his best allies in converting the Indians. They could be a concrete example of what Christians were in life. He constantly appealed to the King for more colonists of the same kind that were arriving. He was, perhaps, over-optimistic in thinking that the virtue of these first simple colonists could be preserved. "It is very easy," he said, "in a new country, where families arrive who are prepared to observe the laws that will be established there, to banish the wicked customs of certain places in France, and to introduce better ones." * He may have been over-optimistic in this belief, but at least his optimism vouches to the excellent conduct of the Norman and Breton colonists who came to New France during the 1630's and 40's.

When Le Jeune had begun to attract the wandering Indians to him by caring for their bellies and bodies, he had suffered from misgivings. He feared they were so carnal, so like animals, that they would not be drawn into any spiritual companionship. He was led to have these misgivings partly because on his winter visit to them they had seemed to him to think only of food and drink. When he taught them the Our Father and came to the "give us this day our daily bread," an Indian had grunted that it should read "give us

* Thwaites, vol. vii, p. 272.

this day moose meat." Father Le Jeune had taken this remark seriously, not realizing that it was one of those laconi-
cisms of the Algonquians, a deliberate expression of age-
sharpened irony. He had decided too quickly that the Algonquians were devoid of spirituality. But now he apologized
for this. He acknowledged his mistake.

The starving tribes did set their thoughts on food : they had
to. But they saw beyond it. They saw the Jesuits beyond it.
They saw Le Jeune, and came to him with an affection not
given to a mere purveyor of food. But, most of all, they
recognized the supernatural mission of the nuns. The nuns
to them were like people descended from heaven. They received from the nuns, earthly things : sagamité (a kind of
maize meal), and medical salves, bandages and potions ; but
the things they received came with a heavenly savor. The
contemplative in the Algonquian Indians perceived in the
nuns something they could not account for. By way of
grotesque compliment, sometimes even the men tried to imitate nuns in dress. The nuns had made God's mercy visible
to them.

As a result an Algonquian here, an Algonquian there, asked
for baptism. They began so to ask even before the nuns arrived, and already there was an Indian congregation for the
little chapel on the St. Charles River, Notre Dame des Anges.
But after the nuns arrived the interest in the Christian Faith
(the prayer as the Indians called it, of the White Men) increased greatly. Far and wide in the woods the Indians
talked about it.

As soon as these converts, in spite of their patient incredulity, had become Christian, they began to show a surprising comprehension of their new religion. They in no way associated it with material comfort. To the edification of the missionaries they insisted, for instance, on being allowed to fast in Lent, even though the missionaries, knowing they were so often starving, dispensed them from so doing. This was a great lesson for Father Le Jeune who had supposed they thought only of their bellies. More than that, certain of the Indians showed a real desire for perfection. "Mortify me," said the Algonquin Ignatius, a convert from the region of Three Rivers, "mortify me in public, so that those who wish to be baptized may persuade themselves that one must exercise virtue when one is a child of God." *

Some of the Indians chose to settle down near Quebec and Three Rivers, and become agricultural. Sillery, their station near Quebec, had in the early 1640's about half as large a population as Quebec itself. But most of the Algonquians had a scorn of sedentary habits, and though not averse to becoming Christians they did not wish to become French. They visited the various missions from time to time : that of St. Joseph at Sillery, that of Notre Dame de la Conception at Three Rivers, and the chapel at Tadoussac ; but most of the year they wandered. Concerning the Indians turned sedentary, the Jesuits had little worry : they could be held to the Faith, for they were near the sacraments. Concerning those who wandered the Jesuits began by being more than anxious, but their anxiety was unjustified, for the wanderers held to their Faith with wonderful tenacity. They even spread it.

* Thwaites, vol. XVI, p. 133.

To the astonishment of the Jesuits, they themselves became missionaries.

One tribe in particular astonished the Jesuits in this respect. They were the Attiguamegues, or as the English more conveniently called them, The White Fish Nation. This tribe, the poorest and most primitive of the Algonquians, accepted the Faith as easily as if they immediately recognized in it what they had in their hearts been awaiting for ages. They lived at the head-waters of the St. Maurice River, the river whose three mouths make Three Rivers, and were separated by some mere three hundred miles from the mission at its three mouths; and yet they descended the river annually to the mission in mysterious flotillas of forty canoes, seeking not food, but instruction in the Faith and ultimately baptism. Such was the innocence of these people that Father Buteux, their Jesuit apostle, who was finally slain with them and for them, literally exclaimed of them :

"It seems as if innocence, banished from the majority of the Empires and Kingdoms of the World, had withdrawn into these great forests where these people dwell. Their nature has something, I know not what, of the goodness of the Terrestrial Paradise before sin had entered it. Their practices manifest none of the luxury, the ambition, the avarice, or the pleasures that corrupt our cities. Since baptism has made them disciples of the Holy Ghost, that Doctor is pleased to be with them ; he teaches them, far from the noise of tribunals and of Louvres ; he has made them more learned, without books, than any Aristotle ever was with his pondrous volumes."

Afterwards he had his word to say of their missionary activity :

"In the third place, in whatever spot or in whatever company they may have been, they have publicly confessed their belief in Jesus Christ ; so that the Hurons who have gone to trade in their country have come back so edified and astonished that our Fathers who are in their villages have given us testimony thereof that is full of consolation. That is not all : they preach the faith so strenuously among the wandering tribes that dwell in the North that those people are attracted by the odor of Christian virtues, and follow them — coming to us to drink, at the source, what they have tasted in the streams. This year we have baptized some as Saint Philip baptized the Eunuch of Queen Candace — after a single conversation — so solid was the instruction they had received, and so holy their preparation by those new preachers of the Gospel. And what seems quite astonishing is, that the women are in no respect behind the men in the performance of that duty. As they are naturally affectionate and more pressing they have less of worldly respect in connection with these strange things, which are so holy and so useful to these people who have remained for so many centuries in the shadows of death." *

The effort to convert the Algonquians was not vain then. Although the baptized could be counted only in hundreds, there were many other other hundreds who were looking towards the Faith of Christians, who in many cases wished to be Christian but feared they could not live by its moral code.

* Thwaites, vol. XXXII, p. 283.

Finally far and wide through the woods the teachings of these tenacious Algonquian converts was carried to the most unexpected places. Tribes who had never seen a priest, like the Abenakis of Maine, heard about priests from other tribes and asked that Black Robes or priests be sent them. The wide influence of the Christian teachings has been well described by Parkman :

"When we look for the result of these missions, we soon become aware that the influence of the French and the Jesuits extended far beyond the circle of converts. It eventually modified and softened the manners of many unconverted tribes. In the wars of the next century we do not often find those examples of diabolic atrocity with which the earlier annals are crowded. The savage burned his enemies alive, but he rarely ate them ; neither did he torment them with the same deliberation and persistency. He was a savage still, but not so often a devil. The improvement was not great, but it was distinct ; and it seems to have taken place wherever Indian tribes were in close relation with any respectable community of white men. Thus Philip's war in New England, cruel as it was, was less ferocious, judging from Canadian experience, than it would have been if a generation of civilized intercourse had not worn down the sharpest asperities of barbarism. Yet it was to French priests and colonists, mingled as they were soon to be among the tribes of the vast interior, that the change is chiefly to be ascribed." *

While the Algonquians were thus learning what was this real secret borne by the White Men from Europe, the Hurons

---

* Parkman, *The Jesuits in North America,* Boston, 1908, pp. 417-18.

thirty days' journey southwest from Quebec were also having their eyes opened, yet in a quite different manner. With them it was not a question of this or that individual Huron becoming impressed by a nun's kindness, or a priest's words, and asking for baptism. The Hurons were Iroquoians, who acted together. Either all Huronia had to turn Christian or none of it could.

In 1639, Fathers de Brébeuf, Davost and Daniel arrived in Huronia, having been brought there, with some unwilling-ness, by the Hurons themselves, but they were not treated or considered as teachers of a religion. They were simply for-eign ambassadors. The Hurons wanted to be the middle-men between the French and the Algonquians in the fur-trade. Therefore it was necessary for them to maintain friendship with the French. At Champlain's request, there-fore, they had brought the missionaries back with them from Quebec in their canoes.

As ambassadors to Huronia, the Jesuits were allowed to build their chapel and to practise their religion, but there was no thought of anyone accepting it. Very often the Huron wise-men would discuss the Christian Faith with the French Jesuits and would express their appreciation of it. Yes, it was a wonderful religion, a wonderful religion for the French. They, the Iroquoians, had their own religion. It was a part of them.

Even though the Jesuits could be thankful that they were allowed to lodge among the Hurons at all, and to talk with them, and to visit them from long-house to long-house daily, it was not a privilege that excited and spurred them on with the sense of impending triumph. There seemed to be no promise ahead. They were not even in any position to win the gratitude of the Hurons by material favors. In the matter of food, the Hurons had as much to eat as they, and were not at all like the starving Algonquians. The Hurons were Iroquoians who cultivated their fields and had a surplus of corn or maize, which they sold to the Nipissings and other Algonquian tribes, who lived improvident about them.

During three whole years in Huronia the Jesuits could not congratulate themselves that they had made any visible progress toward converting the Hurons. They could console themselves very spiritually that secretly they had baptized some ninety dying infants. Otherwise they had to find their joy in learning to be patient, and fortunately their leader, de Brébeuf, was patience itself. He asked for more Jesuits from France but he begged that they be not impatient men. He wanted men who could wait affably.

And the waiting, though it was a waiting for conversions, was not a waiting for everything else. Progress, definite progress, was being made into the hearts, into the society of the Hurons. Brébeuf and his companions were becoming Hurons. Day by day they were becoming more respected and more taken for granted. If they were not over-night changing the Hurons into Christians, they were changing their own Christian French selves into Christian Huron selves. Deliberately they were doing this, for they knew that some one's patience would give out some day, and in that day they wished to have some rights in Huronia. They did not wish to be still such outsiders that the medicine-men, who were

naturally jealous of them, could stand up and say, "These are
mere Frenchmen, these are not of us." In affability, in patience, in humility they bowed themselves to the learning of
Huron customs, and to the following of Huron etiquette.
The greatest of all matters of etiquette was the proper use of
the Huron tongue, the mere speaking of which was in itself
a ceremony.

It was very difficult to gain even a verbal knowledge of the
Iroquoian tongue in a life-time, for it required great powers
of memory to gather in its innumerable words, and great
alertness to be able to make use of its elaborate structure.
Like the Algonquian tongues it showed great sensitiveness to
individual impressions. In English, I use the same word *go*
whether I say I am going across the street, or across the river,
or somewhere to see a friend, or am going somewhere for a
few minutes or for good and all. Not so among the Iroquoians. They had and have, for instance, a different word
for *go* to suit every motive and every manner of the goer. A
Frenchman being used to using the French word for *go* and
to coloring it with some adverb, or purpose clause, was bound
to make innumerable mistakes, which, curiously enough, were
not laughed at by the Hurons as similar mistakes were by
the Algonquians, but which were nevertheless a sufficient
mark that those who made them were not really of the long-
house, were outsiders.

It was also difficult to learn Huron grammar, for it was
extremely elaborate, more elaborate than the Greek, something like the Basque. Of many possible examples of its
complication let us give one. In most languages that we are

used to, we have only eight forms of the present tense: I see, thou seest, he sees, she sees, etc. In Greek, of course, there is the dual with two other forms : "we two see" and "they two see." But such is the complexity of Iroquoian that each present tense has fifteen forms. Not only are there duals in it, but the duals have their various shades of meaning. It made a difference whether one said : *tiatkahtos* (that is, *we two see, thou and I*), or *iakiatkahos, (we two see, he and I)*.* Brébeuf had been studying the language for ten years, but he was still adding to the richness of his dictionary, still puzzling as to the true analysis of its grammar.

But in order to be a real Huron it was necessary to be able to do more than to use the right word in its right form. A special power of poetic diction had to be learned, in which the choice of an illuminating metaphor had to be made. The Iroquoians were and are expert in metaphors. Recently, in 1934, in the Iroquois settlement opposite Montreal, from which Father Chauchetière, whom we encountered in the first chapter, wrote his letter, a celebration † was held during which the Canadian statesman largely responsible for the building of the new bridge from Lachine to their settlement was honored and given a name. The Iroquois mind hit on the right figure of speech to describe what manner of man he who built a bridge was. No, he was not one who stretched iron

---

* Hale, *Iroquois Book of Rites,* p. 108.
† The ceremony was the ordination of Michael Karhaienton (Michael of the Woods), a Mohawk, as priest, on July 1st, 1934. Known now as Father Jacobs S.J., he has been all kindness in giving me information concerning his people. There are still over 2,000 Indians at Caughnawaga.

over waters, or who made a road through the air. Most essentially he was "he who joins lands together." Such he was called. The Iroquois were direct in their metaphors as the Hebrew were, and trusted in metaphorical force. They had never been affected by the logic of the Greeks. Not only did they delight in metaphors but they delighted in the profusion of them. Their speeches were explosive and ejaculatory and chaotic with them. To talk with metaphors as the Hurons talked, was not something which Jesuits, trained to a sober use of the discursive and judicial French of the seventeenth century, could come by without some practise.

And, not only that, the Jesuits could not simply trust to their poetic inventiveness to find their own metaphors. They had to pay a respect to the Huron past in their metaphors. It was necessary to be able to use the traditional metaphors of the Iroquoians, to speak in formulas, which though they recalled the past yet added some variation which freshened the thing remembered. This was not a manner unique to the Iroquoians : most people, among whom an oral tradition is strong, practise it. Even Our Lady followed it when she chanted her Magnificat. During the years 1635 and '36, Brébeuf and his companions, talking day in day out with the Hurons, and constantly being interrupted by them, and having their privacy destroyed by them, learned to use the Iroquoian phrases.

And then the storm burst. It was the Hurons who lost their patience, and the reason they lost it was that a plague had fallen on them, which they were convinced had come from the Jesuits. It was a plague of influenza, which lasted among them for three years and destroyed at least a third of them. If the Jesuits had really caused such a plague then they surely deserved death.

It must be acknowledged that they were not hasty in putting the blame on the Jesuits. Their medicine-men had long been warning them against harboring these Black Robes : they were magicians, wicked magicians. Some Huron parents could well believe this, for they remembered that before their children had died, a Jesuit had seemed to make a strange gesture — the half-perceived sign of the cross — over them. Then the Algonquians between Huronia and Quebec, some of whom wished to be themselves middle-men in the fur-trade, and who wished therefore to break the friendship between the French and the Hurons, spread lying tales about how the Jesuits had claimed to be bringing death to the Hurons. Finally the Hurons had the testimony of their own senses, their own inductive method. Not a single Jesuit died, but everywhere the presence of the Jesuits made Hurons die. And furthermore was this not significant ? In 1638, early in the summer, the first adult Huron was baptized by the missionaries. Immediately he and his wife and his daughter and his brother-in-law, and his niece all died. The evidence was conclusive. In a council held at Ossassané, where de Brébeuf and four other Jesuits were living their ambassadorial life, it was decided that the Jesuits were to be put to death. Even de Brébeuf's best friends, of whom he had many, voted for his death. It was for the common good.

At this point Brébeuf won the battle, and solely by his

patience. At the council which had condemned him he had been allowed to speak in his own defense. He had claimed this right not as an ambassador, but as a Huron. He had spoken like a Huron, proving by Huron reasoning that inasmuch as no charm had been found — no material charm — there was absolutely no proof, not in Huron philosophy, that he had acted as a malevolent sorcerer. As soon as, in spite of his defense (to which no one dared reply), he was condemned, he accepted the decree, and, still acting as a Huron, invited his fellow-Hurons to his Death Feast. Again he was within his Huron rights, and the Hurons came to hear such a speech as an Iroquoian was entitled to make as a vaunting before he died. They listened to Brébeuf's vaunting : it was not the vaunting of his own prowess that he made, but that of the puissance of God. Yet it was a speech which could be recognized and accepted by the Hurons as a Huron speech.

From that moment on the situation at Huronia was completely changed. The decree, to be sure, was not rescinded, but neither was it carried out. Although any Huron had the right to carry it out, no one did. Public opinion had accepted the citizenship in Huronia of the Jesuits. Thus the Jesuits lived on, and the toleration which allowed them to live on gave the Christian religion a right to inhabit the Huron long-houses. This acknowledgment of such a right was tantamount to dooming to death the Huron religion, which owed its sanctity to its inseparable relation with Huron culture. Once it was acknowledged that Huron culture could entertain another religion, the Huron religion had fallen from a great height. Its prestige was gone. All that could now speak for it was its own marks of holiness. The Hurons had always been ready to acknowledge the sublimity of the Christian religion, and now that it was possible for them to hold it, so much the better.

It is true that the medicine-men resented bitterly this change, for under the old religion they had played a prominent part. They had not been priests, for the nearest thing to priests among the Iroquoians had been the elders, but they had been scientists — false scientists, magicians if you wish, but scientists — and as such had occupied a position not dissimilar to that of scientists in our modern society who speak with prestige even on religious subjects, and who live to the public, if not like saints, at least like beings of rare benignity. Now that the Christian priests had a status in the community, the preëminence of these near-scientists was threatened, for the priests were not only priests, but they were truer scientists than the medicine-man : they could wind up clocks that ticked and told the hour, and could predict the workings of the great clock of the sky — its eclipses of sun and moon. The medicine-men were ready to try every means to discredit the Christian Faith, and every means they did try, but their opposition lacked efficacy simply because the Jesuits were holier than they. The Huron elders, praising the good old times to Brébeuf, lamented that the medicine-men were not what they used to be : they neglected "retreats" and "fasting." Thus the medicine-men did not carry the community with them.

Therefore the toleration of Christianity brought spectacular results. Almost immediately fifty Hurons who had long wanted to be Christians but could not conceive how they could be both Hurons and Christians, asked for baptism, and were publicly baptized. Among these were some who gave the missionaries a great hope in the future intellectual quality of the Huron Christians. Joseph Chihwatenhwa learned how to read and write. He had an eagerness to learn about his Faith scholastically, which went parallel with his zeal for prayer. He asked to be allowed to make a week's retreat with the Jesuits in their residence and was so allowed. But quite as remarkable as the literacy of Joseph was the spiritual quality of those who were not called to literacy, but who were surprising in their more Iroquois way. The old pride of the Iroquois, once it had become baptized, turned into a firm resolution to keep the Christian Law. The Iroquoian courage, the Iroquoian readiness to play a part, took on Christian form.

The Iroquoians had shown a great power of self-control even over their thoughts. This was not spontaneous, it was a matter of training. In their dances they taunted and insulted one another, and though they answered one another with counter insults, were never allowed to lose their tempers. They were schooled from childhood to hide their emotions and, more than that, to be able to swing their thoughts to what they wished to concentrate their attention on. Thus they would chant in their sufferings. Now they began to make Christian ejaculations in the place of their chants and to think on God and on paradise.

Some of the Indians thus kept themselves in a constant state of prayer. René Tsondihouanne was asked by one of the Jesuits how many times a day he thought of God during a journey which he had just taken. "Only once," he replied very simply, "but it was from morning to night." The Father asked him whether that conversation with God took place mentally. "Not at all," he said. "I find it better to speak to Him, and thus I am less easily distracted." *

Weakness was not a trait of the Iroquoians. They were merciless to their own weaknesses. They developed their indomitable wills. As Christians this development continued : "While I was returning from a certain village," said a convert woman, "it occurred to me to say my rosary on the way ; but the cold and the discomfort caused me by a piercing wind that blew in my face, led me to give way to the promptings of the flesh, when it suggested that I should defer saying my beads until after I had arrived. When I entered the cabin, I found a bright fire burning and my flesh said to my soul : 'Warm thyself first, and afterwards thou shalt go and say thy beads in the church more comfortably.' Immediately I detected the ruse of the devil, who wished me to lose a portion of the merit that I might gain ; and I replied to my flesh : 'It is too much to have obeyed thee once ; thou must obey in thy turn ; let us go and pray and we will warm ourselves afterwards.' " †

It must not be thought, however, that all Huronia became saintly or even Christian, in 1638, or in 1639, or in any year following. There was great hostility still to the Christian way of life, but generally it was the worst element that remained anti-Christian. It was not the noblest among the

* Thwaites, vol. xxxiii, p. 179.
† Thwaites, vol. xxxiii, p. 173.

Hurons who threw an arm torn from an Iroquois victim into the long-house of the missionaries in 1638 and invited them to eat it. Most of the better type of Hurons admired the Christian "prayer," and its laws, even if they did not wish immediately to become Christian. All that kept them from baptism was a fear that they could not live according to the Christian marriage laws. These latter Hurons were very numerous. The pride of the Hurons, which made them want to live up to their obligations, hindered any great numerical success of the missionaries.

Yet, even then, the hopeful attitude of Father Jerome Lalemant, who succeeded Father de Brébeuf as superior in Huronia after the Death Feast, was warranted. He it was who made the grand plans for Huronia, established a Jesuit capital for it : the fort and central residence of Ste. Marie, a building, permanent, cement-based, ready to be surrounded by Huron villages. He it was who had an orderly census taken of the Huron inhabitants of the region, and who gave to each village its saint's name, and who established chapels far and wide, as if preparing for a future kingdom. He it was who, in 1640, sent Father Jogues and Raymbault to Lake Superior. He saw no reason why Huronia should not become the centre of a vast territory in which slowly the Algonquian tribes surrounding it could be made sedentary. As the Jesuits in South America were at this time establishing in Paraguay their famous Reductions, so he in North America would establish his.

If his plans seemed grandiose there, let us remember that the Paraguayan Reductions, before they were confiscated by the commercial profiteers, contained over a hundred thousand Christian Indians, and had twelve colleges and one university — all among Indians less civilized than the Hurons. There was nothing impossible about Father Lalemant's dreams. Before he left Huronia the converts were coming in at the rate of a thousand a year, and the villages were clustering round his capital, and the Algonquians of the surrounding districts were becoming sedentary. Huronia was on the verge of becoming a vast Indian Commonwealth with such men as Joseph Chihwatenhwa at its head, the Jesuits at its side, and with the French flag fluttering at its ramparts.

CHAPTER VI

APPARENT FAILURE

But an era of disasters now set in, which those who distrust
spiritual men as being always unwise in terrestrial affairs,
can say is exactly what was to be expected. Had not these
French with thoughts in the sky made disaster inevitable by
their lack of military strategy ? They had established in New
France two missions : one at Quebec, the other thirty days'
journey away at Georgian Bay, Huronia. To go from one to
the other there was but one path : the St. Lawrence River.
If that path were severed by an enemy, then New France
had its back broken. And south of that path lay an enemy
of enemies, the Iroquois.

Personally I should hesitate to attribute this situation to the
lack of military strategy of the French, either to that of the
Hundred Associates or of Champlain — who was a canny
soldier — or of the French Jesuits even. The French in
Canada did not have an army nor riches behind them, and
they had to do the best they could under very difficult circumstances. Champlain had been blamed for antagonizing
the Iroquois as he did when he fired an arquebus at them on
Lake Champlain in 1609, killing two of them at one discharge.
But Champlain did not really make the Iroquois his enemies.
They were his enemies because he was friendly to the Hurons

and Algonquians, whom he had to be friends with, for he lived among them, and could protect himself from them only by an army of a dozen men. Because the Iroquois were enemy, the French were unable to establish missions here and there along the St. Lawrence. It had not been safe to establish colonies between Three Rivers and Huronia, and that is the reason why these two centers of French influence were so far apart. In other words, the French of New France were not so much lacking in military sense as ready to take chances.

But this is certain : they were taking a chance, for their position did invite disaster. Not only could New France be cut in two, but no one of the two halves could live without the other. Quebec was not only a mission but a colony, yet it was not a self-supporting colony. It lived by the furs that came down the St. Lawrence River. If the St. Lawrence were barred to them, then the colony was bankrupt. There were not enough pious contributions coming from France to run both a mission and a colony. Huronia was not a colony. Neither was it a French trading-post. It was a Huron clearing-house for furs, and a Jesuit mission. As a Huron clearing-house it lost its importance unless the St. Lawrence pathway was kept open. As a mission, it was helpless, for the Jesuits could not well get along without communication with France, even though they grew their own wheat and could make their own altar-wine.

All that was needed to ruin New France was that an enemy should close the St. Lawrence, and the surprising thing is that the Iroquois had not long since done it, for they were so placed that it required very little energy so to do. They had

the strategic position of a small boy who stands half-way between two cities, with no one looking on, who has but to take
out his shears and cut the telephone wires of communication.
But the truth is that up till 1640 the Iroquois were on the
defensive. A hundred years back they had been driven down
from the St. Lawrence by the Algonquians. And of late in their
battles against their own kin, the Hurons, they had come out
second-best. The addition of the French strength with its
cannon and arquebuses to that of their already over-powerful
opponents did not dispose the Iroquois to do other than stay
in the background. For the sake of gaining victims for their
war-god, and also for the glory of their name, they did send
war-parties north, but they were not parties that planned any
campaign.

Probably no campaign would ever have been waged at all
except for the fur-trade. For over a hundred years there had
been rivalry among the Indians of Canada as to who should
be the middle-men between other Indians, who killed the fur-
bearing animals, and the French who bought the furs, and
who paid for them with such wonderful things as kettles,
and hatchets, and — when the bargaining was fierce — brandy.
In this rivalry the Iroquois had been left out, until the Dutch
arrived at the mouth of the Hudson River. Then the Iroquois
made up for lost time. They thrust aside the Algonquian
Mohicans who had first bargained with the Dutch, and began
to bargain themselves, bargaining so astutely that they forced
the Dutch to sell them arquebuses and gun-powder.

This indiscretion of the Dutch gave the Iroquois a power
which the French had pretty much kept from the Algonquians

and Hurons. Hitherto the Iroquois had fought in close forma-
tion, wearing cotton and wooden armor. They were clever
enough, these inventors of the League, to change their tactics
absolutely, now that they had fire-arms. They gained and
felt their superiority. Not only would they be the middle-
men with the Dutch, but they would be the middle-men with
the French. Or, at least, they would divert down to Manhattan Island all furs hitherto going to Quebec. They had
only to close the St. Lawrence. Recently a good opportunity
had come for closing it. The Hurons had lost half their population by the plague. The French — well the French did not
venture forth as they did in Champlain's day ; and besides
they were so few, and so cautious. Yes, they were wisely
cautious. So the Iroquois struck, and the effect of their striking was soon evident.

The years 1633 through 1637 had been fat years for the
beaver-trade in New France. The company, which had
bought for 10,000 livres the trading rights for five years from
the Hundred Associates made three hundred thousand "livres" *
during those years.† But the next three years were lean, and
by 1640 there was not only no profit being made by anyone,
there was no trade going on at all. The Iroquois had put an
end to it. Coming up towards Canada by Lake Champlain
they had the custom of arriving on the St. Lawrence by what
was then called the River of the Iroquois, but which was
later called and is now called the Richelieu River. Once on

---

* A French "livre" was equivalent to twenty cents, not to an English
pound.
† See Harold A. Innes, *The Fur Trade in Canada,* 1930, p. 37.

the St. Lawrence they hid on the islands of Lake St. Peter, into which expanse the river broadened between Three Rivers and Montreal, and there they waylaid the canoe caravans. Thus in 1640 there was no fur-trade. In 1641 there was still less. New France was being strangled.

This was a plight not pleasant either for the colony and trading-post at Quebec, or for its adjunct, Three Rivers. It was painful in a different way for Huronia, for it isolated Huronia from the entire world. Unless the situation were mended, New France could not go on. And how could the situation mend ? Montmagny, the Governor — Onontio — might possibly muster a hundred men from Quebec and Three Rivers ; but he was no such fool as to march out with them against the Iroquois. All he could do was to wait.

In the late summer of 1641 something happened which averted inevitable disaster : a double thing happened. Forty soldiers arrived from Cardinal Richelieu, and with them the promise of ten thousand "écus." * That was the first thing, and a very heartening one. But the more extraordinary arrival was that of a ship from France with forty men and four women, who came to found a colony at Montreal. The name of the company which sent them out which had bought the island was the "Associates of Our Lady of Montreal." They had no idea of making any money, and I might say also that they had no idea of what they were doing, or of the rôle Providence was going to give them.

They had crossed the ocean in sublime folly, primarily in order to establish a hospital at Montreal, where as Parkman

* An écu was worth three "livres," that is, sixty cents.

said, there was no one to hospitalize. They knew nothing of the Iroquois war. They certainly had no conception that, if they did found and fortify Montreal, they would be establishing a fortress, extraordinarily strategic, just behind the backs of the Iroquois. Yet unwittingly they came to do that very thing. Dauversière, of whom I have already spoken as an example of a visionary of this time, had long since dreamed of founding his Montreal Hospital, and now he was at last founding it. In order to protect it he had somehow enlisted in his enterprise one of the canniest soldiers in France, Maisonneuve, who had been a soldier since his teens, and who still loved to fight, but who had said that he wished to use his sword only to serve his King, Christ.

Montmagny, who was no skeptic, had his misgivings about this apparently heavenly expedition, much as he welcomed it. He advised Maisonneuve not to take possession of the island until the following spring,— the winter was too near — advice which Maisonneuve listened to. The forty colonists passed the winter at Quebec, they and the four women, who were to found the hospital. In the spring they started for Montreal and founded it, and built a fort there which they held in the face of never-ceasing Iroquois harassings which lasted for fifty years. Montmagny, as they parted from Quebec, wished still to bring the expedition a bit nearer earth, and offered to pay Maisonneuve a salary. Maisonneuve refused it. Of all the colonies founded in Canada, or possibly in the world, Montreal was the oddest.

The year 1642 began therefore with a new courage at Quebec. Now the blockade could be broken. With Montreal on one flank of the Iroquois parties, and Three Rivers on the other, perhaps the raids could be controlled. Furthermore, Montmagny had his forty men from the Cardinal whom he would station at the mouth of the Richelieu River. He would build there a fort, Fort Richelieu. The year 1642 seemed to some like the end of troubles, like the saving of New France.

In this new optimism the first real canoe flotilla which had dared go up or down the St. Lawrence for three years, started out from Quebec in July to bring supplies to Huronia. Fort Richelieu had not yet been founded, but the ships had been sailing up to Montreal, and the river seemed clear of Iroquois, and the flotilla was to be strongly armed. Fifteen canoes started off, containing sixty men, three of them Frenchmen, the rest Indians : Huron converts and Algonquians. In the party was one girl Thérèse, a Huron who had been studying at Quebec with the Ursulines. So confident was Montmagny that better days had come, that he dared send even her.

But better days had not come, the flotilla was waylaid in the Lake of St. Peter, by Iroquois so well-equipped with fire-arms that the very bombardment they made surprised the Algonquins into turning their canoes, and speeding back to-wards Three Rivers. The canoes containing the White Men and the Hurons were captured with their occupants, and there ensued a terrible story of torture and heroism, which is fa-miliar to all who have heard of St. Isaac Jogues* or St. René Goupil, for these two were among the captives. Both of these men were led to the Mohawk village of Ossernenon, which

* For all the details concerning Father Jogues and his captivity see by Francis Talbot, S.J., *Saint Among Savages*, New York, 1935.

was the easternmost gate of the Iroquois League, twenty miles southwest of the present Albany, on the Mohawk River, and were there slashed and gnawed and beaten. Treated for a while as victims to be sacrificed to Areskoi, they were both at last by various women claimed as adopted children. Goupil, in spite of this adoption, was killed by a brave who saw him making the Sign of the Cross over an Indian child. Father Jogues did not die — not this time. He escaped through the help of the Dutch, visited Manhattan Island, was hailed there somewhere near Wall Street as "martyr, martyr" by a little Lutheran lad * and finally with mangled hands returned to France. The story of Jogues reminds us that in 1642 better days had not come.

Nor did better days come in 1643, nor in 1644. It was in 1644 that Father Vimont who had succeeded Father Le Jeune as superior at Quebec made the jesting remark that the French colonists had to live cloistered lives within their stockades, just as if they were monks, without the gift of prayer. But the whole situation could evoke tears as well as laughter, and one of the sorrowful aspects of it was the dispersion of the Algonquians just as they were beginning to crowd about the French and to become sedentary. The Iroquois when they crept in their raids round the stockades of Fort Richelieu, or the equally fort-like defenses of Three Rivers and Quebec, were concerned not only with capturing Frenchmen, but with massacring and making flee to the bleakest regions of the

---

* Buteux, *Narré de la prise du Père Isaac Jogues*. Copy at College Sainte-Marie, Montreal (of which a translation was printed in "The Pilgrim of Our Lady of the Martyrs," January-December, 1896).

North, the Algonquians. Father Vimont writes of the desolation :

"Where eight years ago one could see a hundred wigwams, one now sees scarcely five or six. A chief who once had eight hundred warriors has now but thirty or forty ; and in place of fleets of three or four hundred canoes, we see less than a tenth of that number." *

In 1645, however, once again there was a ray of light. An enterprising Algonquian warrior, Piscaret, had waylaid the Iroquois themselves, and brought home to Quebec some Iroquois captives. Montmagny, using the tone of a conqueror, told the Iroquois he would give them peace if they wanted it, and offered to restore to them safe and sound the captives, whom the Christianized Algonquians had danced about and mocked at, but had not tortured. The Iroquois may possibly have been touched by this kindness to their warriors, or they may have been simply exhausted by the conflict, or they may have wanted to detach the French from their alliance with the Algonquins. Whatever was their motive, all that Montmagny was aware of it, was that, to his amazement and satisfaction, the Iroquois were suing for peace. He was being treated like the victor which he did not so surely feel himself to be.

Peace was thereupon made, and the tokens that were given and the speeches delivered, and the pacts consented to, gave the impression that it was a lasting peace. And as such it was welcomed with jubilation, especially by the French. Sixty Huron canoes came down the St. Lawrence River to Quebec, piled with furs. The French farmers dared once again go

* Cited by Parkman, *Jesuits in North America*, p. 341.

into their fields. They, most assuredly, were happy. And the Iroquois — they too were ready for a rest.

But the peace was broken, and it was Saint Isaac Jogues who was the cause of its breaking, and its breaking came in this way. He, Jogues, had been sent down in the spring of 1646 to the very village where he had suffered and where St. René Goupil had had his head cleft open, to the same Ossernenon, near to the Dutch, from which he had formerly escaped. At Ossernenon he who had once been a victim ready to be sacrificed to Areskoi, was now hailed with admiration because he had been so brave a victim. Ondessonk, as he had come to be called by the Mohawks, was greeted also as an ambassador of peace from Onontio — that is the Great Mountain, the work being a translation of Montmagny. He had come to ratify and confirm the peace. He succeeded.

Yet he knew well that there was a party among the Mohawks which wished for war, and therefore, even though he quitted Ossernenon in the spring of 1646, he left behind him in the village some of his vestments, and some vessels for the celebration of Mass. The June warmth was beginning : it was difficult to carry baggage, and he intended to return. He left this treasure of his buried in a black box.

He did return, but during his absence a summer had intervened, during which the caterpillars had devoured the beans of the Iroquois. The crops had failed. The medicine-men among the Mohawks were convinced, or pretended to be convinced, that the box which Jogues had left behind, his specifically Christian baggage, had been a charm that had brought blight on the Mohawk harvests. So when Father Jogues

made his October excursion back to Ossernenon, it was cut
short by some of the Mohawks — those most impressed by the
medicine-men, who happened to be of the Bear Clan — who
met him half-way, and who led him captive into Ossernenon,
having, before he arrived there, cut off strips of his flesh and
devoured them.   Once arrived at Ossernenon, he had friends
who, mostly of the Turtle Clan, interposed for him, some
of them because of their liking for him, some of them
because they felt they were honor-bound to treat him well.
But nevertheless on October 18th he was murdered, and
martyred — both he and St. John Lalande, the latter a kind of
acolyte, his attendant.

Jogues' death brought war.   Not primarily because it called
for vengeance from the French, but because it released a
diabolic fury in the Iroquois.   Especially in the Mohawks was
it fatal to peace.   The more fiendish among the Mohawks
gained the upper hand, and they behaved in a manner not
even true to Iroquois traditions.   What they did was rather
Anti-Christian than pro-Areskoi.   They did not wait for the
winter to be over before they arrived on the St. Lawrence.
They approached Piscaret, the Christian Algonquian warrior
who had captured some of their number in 1634 and had
treated them well and brought about peace.   They approached
him with show of friendship, for nothing had been said concerning peace coming to an end.   They approached him, and
then from behind slew him.   They desecrated more than
friendship.   They captured a French child near Montreal,
and to show their hatred of Christ, crucified it.   Hitherto the
Iroquois had fought against the French because the French

were allies of their enemies. Now they had a blind desire to exterminate the French. A party of Iroquois set out to attack Three Rivers, seeing that Montreal, because of the skill of Maisonneuve, had proved impregnable. Fort Richelieu had been abandoned. The first thing to do was to destroy the feeblest French settlement, Three Rivers, and the destruction of it seemed possible, and probable, and imminent.

But the Hurons were not reckoned with. The Hurons too had laid their plans. As the Iroquois approached Three Rivers they were ambushed by the Hurons : Three Rivers was saved. The Iroquois had suffered their first real defeat in a decade. Rejoicing broke out among the French, and in them rose a new confidence, one that was founded on the strength of the Hurons. Father Lalemant, it seemed, had really organized Huronia into a strong commonwealth. Its plagues were at an end. It was beginning to act. It could save New France.

Father Lalemant, himself, partook of the confidence. He had lately been transferred to Quebec, there to act as superior of all the Jesuit missions in New France. He was so hopeful of what might come to pass in Huronia, that in the spring of 1638, the spring after the Iroquois defeat, he sent a new detachment of priests to Huronia, and with them twenty-five laymen, men not Jesuits, but most of them men of piety who chose to work without wages, for heavenly reward. The flotilla that carried them up the St. Lawrence River was not intercepted. Truly it seemed as if the Hurons and French were mastering the situation.

But before the French had arrived at Georgian Bay an unexpected disaster had taken place. There was a Huron town,

St. Joseph's, which lay in the southeast corner of Huronia, and which was thus nearest the Iroquois. In it stood a mission chapel, conducted by Father Daniel. St. Joseph's was a place well aware of its proximity to the Iroquois, and it had its palisades for defense against them. But in this particular summer, the defenders of it had no fears. It was they, particularly those of St. Joseph's, who had last year ambushed the Iroquois. This year they would ambush them again, and off to ambush them they had already gone. But the Iroquois, who were much more astute in planning campaigns than the haphazard Hurons, circumvented them, came on the village when it was unprotected, broke down the palisades, slaughtered the old and young, the sick and the women, and slaughtered among them Father Daniel, a Jesuit who had been a dozen years among the Hurons and who had gained somewhat the same prestige as Father de Brébeuf.

This was a very unfortunate blow in itself, and as such was recognized, but its ultimate gravity was not at the time appreciated. It meant obviously that many Hurons, though not many Huron warriors, had been killed. It meant also plainly that a very experienced Jesuit could serve the Hurons no more. Yet it did not at all seem to threaten the existence of Huronia. The Huron morale was still good : the warriors of Huronia were such they could turn the tables on the Iroquois. St. Joseph's was not the capital of the Huronia. The real capital was flourishing.

Ste. Marie, the main Jesuit residence, which played the part of capital, gave even every sign of future grandeur. Merely as a collection of buildings it was impressive. It had its granaries, its houses for hospitality, its barns for cattle — for somehow cattle had been, no one knows how, carried there by the missionaries — its hen-houses, its chapel of course, its ward for the sick. Some of the Jesuits were enough like Vauban to have built at Ste. Marie a fort on much the same style that Vauban was constructing his forts in France. It also had its garrison, consisting even of a half a dozen real soldiers who had been sent out by Richelieu. Ste. Marie was visibly flourishing, and around it the Hurons of Huronia were beginning to gather lovingly and confidently in mission villages. From it as a centre new missions were being sent out to the northern Algonquians and to other Iroquoian tribes to the southwest. St. Joseph could be forgotten when the heart of Huronia was beating so vigorously.

One thing the Hurons should have remembered, and that was the strategy of the Iroquois. The Iroquois of all Iroquoians were most ready to help themselves, and most ready to accept innovations in order to preserve what was essential in their customs. Therefore their deeds could not always be calculated in advance by other Iroquoians. This winter they did something unheard of : they encamped in the snow in the wilderness near Huronia, and while the Hurons were planning their excursions, and were indeed off on them in order to get a start on the Iroquois, the Iroquois dodged through the gap left by St. Joseph's, descended like a thunder-clap — a thunder-clap in March — on a village in the centre of Huronia, almost in sight of Ste. Marie, St. Ignace.

As in the case of St. Joseph's Mission, the warriors were

away. St. Ignace was burned. Near to St. Ignace was another village, so unimportant and so safe that it had not the usual defenses. This was next attacked. Commanding the defenses there, was Father de Brébeuf, Saint Jean de Brébeuf, the affable and patient. Like the Hurons, he did not suspect that a whole Iroquois army had been able to penetrate so far north so soon. Therefore he thought there was a possibility of St. Louis holding out. He bade the women and children to flee, and stood, tall and comforting among the few old men and boys who tried to defend the place, not himself as a warrior but as a friend to the Huron warriors, who could make them fight with a double valor.

But the Iroquois were the whole Iroquois army : a thousand of them. St. Louis fell. Brébeuf and his companion Jesuit, Father Gabriel Lalemant — now Saint Gabriel Lalemant, a nephew of the Father Lalemant who had dreamed of the Commonwealth of Huronia — were captured by the Iroquois, and tortured, and put to death. The number of Jesuits in Huronia was by this disaster diminished by two, and the nine mission villages, within walking distance of Ste. Marie, had been similarly diminished. In place of St. Ignace and St. Louis lay two patches of black ashes still smoking two days later. In place of the two noble living forms of the Jesuits were two bodies horribly and elaborately mutilated. Brébeuf had no heart : it had been torn from his breast and eaten. Lalemant had no eyes : instead there were two charred coals which had been thrust into his eye-sockets. And the Iroquois who had stayed over-night to sacrifice these victims had hidden themselves again. Their force was still intact. They had grown demonic with victory.

Within a month, fifteen other Huron villages had been burned, mostly by the Hurons themselves, in despair. A series of evil coincidences had led the Huron warriors time after time to do exactly the wrong thing. It seemed that the dice were loaded against them. In spite of their bravery, in spite of their superior numbers, they were struck down again and again. Finally those who were still alive, and not yet been captured, begged the Jesuits to take them to a place of safety, to the island of St. Joseph a few miles from the mainland in Georgian Bay. The Jesuits too, therefore, because there was no alternative, burned their residence, and rafted themselves with the Hurons to an island which they did not themselves choose for a resort, and which they should never have allowed themselves to be made to choose.

St. Joseph's Island! It represents the last hope that Huronia might continue, for it was still a part of Huronia. But how forlorn a hope! Before the winter began, the Iroquois in their rage against anything Christian had descended on the missions to the southwest of Huronia, the missions among the Tobacco Nation. One of the mission villages, Saint John's, had gone up in smoke on the eve of the Feast of the Immaculate Conception. Its missionary, Father Garnier, had been shot by an arquebus. Then, in the same December, Father Chabanel on his way from the Tobacco Nation to St. Joseph's Island was also killed. The missionaries with their twenty-five laymen did build a fort on the Island. And they prayed as usual. But the Will of God which they prayed to have done was not making their hope for Huronia, St. Joseph's Island, a well-founded hope. It was not a hope; it was a prison, a prison with little to eat for the prisoners. Starvation changed men's visages, changed men's habits to inhuman habits. The long winter passed like a fearful torture.

The next spring an emaciated regiment of several hundred Hurons, and two score Frenchmen took a trek through an uninhabited country from Georgian Bay down to Montreal. Fortunately they met no large body of the enemy in their path — for the Iroquois, too, were exhausted. They came to Montreal and went on to Quebec. But not even yet had they left misfortunes behind. Scarcely had they settled at Quebec, than one of the Ursuline Sisters, who did the Ursuline's cooking, left some hot coals where she should not have left them. The Ursuline Convent went up in flames on New Year's Eve. Even previous to that, there had not been place to lodge the two score Frenchmen from Georgian Bay. Now there was less space. There was less food. And there were two hundred Hurons to feed.

From a material point of view it is difficult to exaggerate the weight of these blows which had just fallen on New France. True, even though the Ursuline Convent had cost sixty thousand livres, the value of the property destroyed by the Iroquois would seem to us moderns as infinitesimal. Even the number of Hurons and Jesuits killed — and Algonquians too — would not read as worth looking at twice in a history of modern war. But the property destroyed was tremendous in comparison with what property existed, and the amount of

country which suddenly became tenantless was like half of
Europe. All that was left of New France after seventeen
years of really heroic effort was nothing more than three
settlements on the St. Lawrence River : Quebec, Three Rivers
and Montreal. These together contained not a half-thousand
White Men, and each of them was in a perpetual state of
siege. Both as a missionary venture and as a colonizing
venture New France looked as if it had turned into a ridicu-
lous failure. Spiritual France had seemed to have achieved
in New France nothing more than a Quixotic blunder.

Yet it is a complete missing of the point to consider these
disasters simply as so many disasters. Because of the way
in which they were taken, they were translated into something
very different from disasters. Saint Isaac Jogues regretted
exceedingly that he and the convert Hurons were waylaid on
the St. Lawrence River. His body did not enjoy the tortures
that followed after his capture. Yet he tells us that he never
felt anything but love for his captors. They were coming to
God through him. He was suffering in order to bring to
them the help which comes from Heaven. He was their
father, their Black Robe. God was conferring on him an
apostolic honor. He offered his sufferings literally for them,
and made himself love them, as those who suffer for another
can scarcely help loving that other, even in the natural order.
We all of us remember Jogues' action on the platform at
Ossernenon. An Indian woman at her husband's bidding
had bitten off his thumb — his left thumb. Taking the thumb
in his right hand he held it up to God. "I then taking my
cut-off thumb in my other hand, offered it to Thee, my living

and true God, mindful of the sacrifices which for ten years I had been offering to Thee in the Church." * After Jogues' death Father Lalemant, the superior, referred to Ossernenon even before it was a mission, as the Mission of the Martyrs. Jogues had taken his disaster as an opportunity.

Similarly the disaster at St. Joseph's Mission where Father Daniel had been killed was to Father Daniel an opportunity. During the last moments of his life he baptized by aspersion hundreds of Hurons who had put off baptism because they feared they could not keep the laws of Christian life, but who at the menace of life's end wished to die Christians. That was part of his opportunity : the part most evident to him. Martyrdom was in itself an opportunity : an opportunity, with consequences less discernible, but which he knew from old sayings led to a sowing of the seeds of Faith.

The death of Brébeuf has always waked great admiration for his courage, but the admiration has often painted a somewhat false picture of that hero. It has made of him a giant man — as he was — but somewhat too much a mere ox of endurance as he characterized himself in a play of words on his name. In the notes which Brébeuf jotted down in his spiritual retreats at the command of his director we find him not at all the thick-skinned heroic but somewhat insensitive Norman that some have imagined him to be. He was for all his common-sense — or perhaps like Mme. Acarie because of it — singularly sensitive to supernatural visions. He was continually offering himself to Our Lady as a martyr, if God

---

* From Jogues' letter to his Provincial, written in Latin. See Thwaites, vol. XXXIX, p. 175.

thought him worthy of the honor, in order that he might bring Christ to the Indians. In these visions, which he merely related as they appeared to him, without at all claiming them to be supernatural, he had received once the promise from Our Lady that he should have peace. We can think of the peaceful composure of the man as something far more, then, than an easy-going disposition. As for his martyrdom he had had a premonition of it in seeing, while at Mass, himself and some of his companions spotted with blood. His death, therefore, was almost like a direct reply to his prayers, granting not so much a suffering like Our Lord's, but the consummation of his missionary labors, the ultimate bringing of Christ to the long-houses which he had found so hospitable.*

The death of Gabriel Lalemant has its secret which is a more open one. He was a scholarly delicate young man, filled with a zeal to be in every way another Christ even on the Cross, but disturbed by a fear that he was a mere scholar. He was the learning of France offering itself as a sacrifice. The fact that Lalemant suffered longer than Brébeuf, even staying alive over night at his stake of torture, and that he was more obviously in agony, and so much younger, has made his offering more piercing to our hearts. His death was a very tremendous and very evident victory.

One might say that the deaths of each and all of these

---

* I take pleasure in thanking the learned archivist of the Collège Sainte-Marie, Montreal, Père Arthur Mélançon S. J., for having presented to me the type-written copy of "Mémoires touchant la mort et les vertus des Pères Isaac Jogues . . . Jean de Brébeuf . . . ," (a manuscript of 1652), in which (pp. 422-40) are contained the excerpts from Saint Jean de Brébeuf's journal which describes his visions.

Jesuits really brightened each and all of the tragic disasters. The burning of the mission of St. John among the Tobacco People enabled Father Garnier to arrive in Heaven on the Feast of the Immaculate Conception. He was a man who had had to enter the Society of Jesus against the wishes, not of a bad, but of a good family — which had been hard. He was thus singularly detached from the world. He used to say that the Blessed Virgin had herself carried him in her arms into the Society. When he was living among the Hurons, and then among their kin the Tobacco Nation, he used to pray to Our Lady that somehow he might go to the Iroquois. He did go to the Iroquois, though it was not far that he had to go. They had come to St. John to meet him.

The final death — that of Noël Chabanel — sacrificed something even more difficult than a scholar's learning to God ; it sacrificed the repugnance of a civilized European to the barbarism of the Indians. Chabanel could not love — not with his sensibilities — the Hurons. He loathed the Hurons (and the Tobacco People, to whom he was sent as a missionary) as some people loathe a cat or a snake — instinctively. He shrank from them. It was not their wickedness that he abhorred ; it was their filthiness, and, above all, their complete disregard of privacy. He detested and could not learn their language. In his heart he so longed for the refinement of France that he was afraid that he could not hold out, that he might beg to be sent back to France. In his desperation he took an oath of stability which gave him new peace of mind, but enabled him not at all to like the Indians any better. He prayed that he might be accepted as a martyr, but knowing his unworthiness he asked that it might be a hidden martyrdom, one in obscurity—appropriate to him, inglorious. And such a martyrdom he received, alone and from an apostate Huron, and in the depth of the forest, as far as possible, from France.

The Jesuits who had survived could not help but regard the death of their comrades, especially when they saw so near to them—only six miles from Ste. Marie—the mutilated bodies of Brébeuf and Lalemant, as examples of terrible Iroquois cruelty; and yet Father Ragueneau, who was superior in Huronia at the time of the disaster, referred to them as examples also of something else; the triumph of God's love. Thus the disasters were transformed by the Jesuits into a triumph, a triumph for which they had all prayed, and in which on their knees they rejoiced.

One thing they did not pray for was the abandonment of their dearly beloved fortress-residence of Ste. Marie, and for the burning of it that they had to perform themselves. Their only comment as the flames arose in the short June night, however, was: "God has never dwelt so lovingly with us."

Finally when they had returned to Quebec, when all was ruins behind them, and when even at Quebec there had faced them the ruins of the Ursuline Convent, there was no thought of moaning. Extraordinary measures had indeed to be taken by those who conducted the affairs of the colony in order to maintain it. Father Jerome Lalemant sailed for France in the spring to beg for help. A Jesuit, Father Druillettes, was sent to Boston to see if the New Englanders, though Calvinists, would join with Quebec in trying to restrain the Mohawks. But really the extraordinary measures accomplished very little. What really saved the colony, the missions, and likewise New France for France, was the extraordinary — and at the same time very ordinary — Christian spirit of the colonists as a whole. Marie de l'Incarnation wrote a letter to her son on the September after the burning of her convent. It described how the Ursulines had been able to continue. "Monsieur le gouvenor d'Ailleboust and Madame his wife have also assisted us. In fact we have been the object of compassion and of charity to all our friends. The compassion has spread even to the poor ; one of them offered us a napkin, another a shirt, another a cloak. Another gave us a chicken, another eggs and so on. . . . You know the poverty of this country, but the charity there is even greater." *

The taking of their disasters by the colonists — by all the Frenchmen and Frenchwomen — as they were taken, gave to them a triumph which we can well perceive, a kind of consummation to the work of Spiritual France in New France. It was not the kind of triumph that Spiritual France had prayed for, but it was not a vague Quixotic kind of triumph. The French, in spite of the difference of language and of the greater and more exclusive difference in culture which separated them from the Indians, had been capable of pronouncing the name of Christ in a way that could be recognized. They had revealed their secret to the human obstinacy that was living on, tenacious, heroic, and misled, in the North American forests.

* Quoted in Rochemonteix, vol. II, p. 118.

CHAPTER VII

EVENTS AMONG THE IROQUOIS

SPIRITUAL FRANCE may have had its spiritual triumph, but there is no denying that the Iroquois had won a great military victory, and they were now faced with the consequence of it. One consequence of it was that they were puffed up with military pride, and had aroused the hostility of tribes hundreds of miles away from their Long-House. They were, in other words, faced with future wars. The other consequence is of a different order. They had shed the blood of Christians who were glad to shed their blood for them, as Christ had been glad to shed His blood for the whole world. They had entered into a new and quite different relation with the Christian religion.

The former of these consequences was very plain to the eye. During the next three years after the destruction of Huronia the Iroquois were engaged in a series of ruthless and very successful campaigns during which they annihilated and absorbed the Tobacco Nation and the Eries, both of which peoples had previously been as powerful as they. More than this, they harried the French, and captured and slew individual Frenchmen even in the very vicinity of Quebec. They dispersed the Algonquians who were becoming sedentary along the St. Lawrence. They raided as far north as the

Attiguamegues or White Fish people, and in 1652, on the tenth of May, slew among them their apostle, Father Buteux. At one time they even over-reached themselves in attacking the Algonquian wanderers in what is now the state of Michigan ; but in general they met astounding success. They had acquired the habit of success in arms.

The latter consequence — that they had now entered into a new relation with the Christian religion — was harder to see. Various things hinted at it, however. For instance, it was obvious now that the Iroquois had adopted into their Long-House hundreds of Indians, Huron and Algonquian, men and women, who had received the mark of Christians. Some of these became apostate Christians and were much more furious against Christ than the merely pagan Iroquois had ever been. Such had been those, who, when Brébeuf was tied to his stake, threw boiling water on him in mockery of baptism. The most fiendish of the Iroquois who destroyed Huronia and its missions there were Hurons who had been captured and adopted by the Iroquois, and who against the pinch of conscience had given up their Faith. Others of these Christians clung to their Faith secretly, some with tepidity, others with zealous though hidden tenacity. Neither the apostate nor the steadfast Christians could ever become old-fashioned Iroquois.

But much more hidden than this were other events which mysteriously and surely showed that a new day was dawning for the Iroquois. Among these events there is none more hidden, and none more mysterious, than the completely unre-marked growing up among the Iroquois of a little girl who was born at the now famous Ossernenon in 1656, ten years after Saint Isaac Jogues had in that village suffered martyrdom.

This child came to be called Tekakwitha.* It was a usual name. She was a usual child. Her birth was not attended by any extraordinary events. Neither was her childhood exceptional. Her father was a Mohawk sachem, her mother was an Algonquin captive.† This was not an extraordinary combination, for the Mohawk sachems liked to take wives from not among the Iroquois : the Iroquois woman had too much tendency to command, whereas the Algonquian women were brought up to be more docile. It was tragic when in the small-pox epidemic of 1660 both her father and mother and little brother died of the disease, but the tragedy was a familiar one, and could be mended after an Iroquois fashion. Tekakwitha's uncle became her father. The name she would have had for her father and uncle, would have been the same any way : uncle. She was an orphan, but among uncivilized people orphans have a lot often much less pitiable than among the civilized.

It is true that one thing came near to making her exceptional at Ossernenon : her mother was a Christian, one of

---

* The two chief sources for our knowledge of the details of Tekakwitha's life are the lives of her by Fathers Chauchetière and Cholenec, written in 1695 and 1717, the former of which is the more intuitive, the latter the more analytical. Only the former has been published.

† Father Mélançon of Collège Sainte-Marie, Montreal, unique in his familiarity with the records of this period, tells me that there is no record of any Iroquois raid on the Algonquins in the years preceding Tekakwitha's birth, but that there is record of an Iroquois hunting-party having in a most unusual way joined with an Algonquin one. If the marriage of Tekakwitha's mother to her father resulted from this amity, it makes the birth of Tekakwitha beautifully symbolic.

those Algonquins from whom is derived the word Algonquian. She had lived near the Mission of the Immaculate
Conception at Three Rivers and had been there baptized.
Had the child of this Christian mother also been baptized it
would have made the child in 1656 something of an oddity
at a place where there were no baptized children, and where
the Christian Faith was more mocked at than in any other
of the Iroquois villages. But Tekakwitha's mother did not
take it upon herself to perform the baptism, any more than
any other captive Christian Indians would have thought of
baptizing their children. It was something to be left to the
priests, and no priest had visited Ossernenon since two years
before Tekakwitha's birth. Thus, although Tekakwitha's
mother was a pious Christian who prayed for her daughter
at her own death, yet she left the daughter unmarked by any
sacrament, and could pass on to her nothing more lasting
than such a memory as a child of four could retain. Tekakwitha may never have been able to forget a Christian gentleness in her mother, but even then by her mother's death, she
lost — so it seemed — the last chance of having an exceptional
destiny of any kind. She could not even be a lone Christian
at Ossernenon.

Similarly as Tekakwitha grew up, she had every appearance of becoming an average Mohawk maiden. Owing to
her own attack of the small-pox she was badly pock-marked
in her face. Also her eyes had been weakened by the disease.
Yet if these were defects, they were more than made up for by
her good Iroquois skill in making decorations of wampum,
and in sewing moccasins of leather. She was strong enough

to perform the manual labor which the Iroquois women had to do, like cutting wood for the fires, and helping in the fields. She was obedient also, and cheerful, and caused little concern. She was a conformist in all that was best in old Iroquois etiquette. She was not even a rebel against Iroquois taboos.

Tekakwitha's first knowledge of the French and of their Black Robes came through hearsay. The first words she ever heard may very well have been the news that the Onondagas who owned the capital city of the Iroquois League had invited some of the Black Robes to live with them. The cause for the invitation had been no friendliness to the religion of the Black Robes, but a desire on the part of the Onondagas to share in the trade with the French. This incensed the Mohawks who preferred to do the trading themselves through the Dutch, and who detested the religion of the Black Robes. They did all they could to put an end to the sojourn of the priests among the Onondagas, especially when a hundred Onondagas became Christians, and they finally did put an end to it. Tekakwitha may have heard the grunts of satisfaction when this peace with the French came to an end, and when the war was resumed.

In 1666, when she was ten years old, she had a very intimate experience of this war. In that year a French army appeared before her village, which was no longer Ossernenon — for Ossernenon had because of the pollution of the plague in 1660 been moved to Kanawaké a mile or two up the Mohawk River — and frightened her people into abandoning it. She and her kin fled into the cold leaves of an autumnal forest on a very black night which was blacker and more dramatic than most nights, in that thunder, lightning and October sleet played in unwonted combination in its sky. The night became even more different from most nights when up into its swift clouds, and athwart them, streamed in the wind the flames of her village which the French army had set fire to.

Yet dire as was the loss of the village and its supplies of corn, the Mohawks had done well in not trying to defend its triple Iroquoian palisades, for the army that marched against it was a European army fully equipped with European instruments of war, against which wooden palisades were as matchwood. This army did not represent the authority of the Hundred Associates but that of the King of France, the great king who made himself almost a god, Le Roi Soleil, Louis XIV.

Up to the year 1663 the Associates had by their own efforts maintained New France, and had received from no king of France any great aid. In some respects they had lamentably failed. They had found it very costly to transport colonists across the ocean. It had cost the English a half million French livres to bring over the thousand English colonists to Massachusetts Bay in 1630,* and the planting of French farmers in Canada was even more expensive. The system of granting of land to various rich Frenchmen, on the condition that they take over the cost of transport of colonists to their fiefs or "seigneuries," had not been a complete success. At

---

* See E. Salone, *La Colonisation de la Nouvelle France*, p. 49.

any rate none of Richelieu's hopes had been fulfilled. By 1663 there were in Canada at the most 2500 * colonists. In other respects the Associates had done better than could have been expected of them : with the few colonists that they had they had made every farm-house a fort, and every nunnery even, and had saved New France from extinction by the Iroquois.

By the year 1663, however, the Hundred Associates were helpless through lack of funds. Therefore they had been glad to let the new king, who had just come of age, take from them their rights and their obligations. The King, when he accepted their forfeiture, did not keep all the rights in his own hands — not at first. He tried granting the trading privileges to still another company, that of "Les Indes Occidentales," which guarded them ineptly and unprofitably for only ten years. But even then he was from now on in New France the real master. It was he who must protect it from the Iroquois. He had sent to Quebec, therefore, in 1665 a real army, a kingly army : six hundred trained soldiers, the Carignan-Sallières Regiment, under a competent commander who had fought victoriously against the Turks and the Dutch, the Marquis de Tracy. It was this regiment increased to an army of over a thousand with Canadian irregulars which had arrived at Kanawaké.

The arrival of this army at the fortresses of the proud Mohawks announces definitely that a new era had begun in Canada, in which spiritual motives should play a less important part than before the King intervened. At the same

---

* Salone, *La Colonisation de la Nouvelle France,* p. 109.

time this expedition led by de Tracy was not in any sense in defiance of spiritual principles, nor was it an expedition that Montmagny in the days of the Hundred Associates would not have been glad to make had he possessed the power. Even with a force of one hundred and fifty men — so he said — he would have marched against the Iroquois castles. It did not set forth until every means had been tried of bringing the Iroquois to terms. Tracy was no fire-eater. He was seventy years old and knew what war was. But he had found that the Mohawks would not make peace, and were not afraid of him. He marched therefore in October, 1666, down to the Mohawk River, and there burned, one after the other, the three villages of the Mohawks. Then back he marched, dragging his two cannon after him, without having once let loose their dreaded thunder.

The burning of the villages did not arouse an unrelenting rage in the Iroquois. They were used to keeping their temper. They did not in the least take it as something unjustifiable. It was merely a part of the game of warfare. They accepted a defeat from the French as they dealt defeats to others, and, recognizing it, they sent emissaries to Quebec to arrange for an ending of hostilities, for what they called a "burying of the hatchet," meaning thereby not really our European hatchet nor their tomahawk, which was a recent importation, but, much more ancient, the war-club.

In the real peace that ensued the Black Robes arrived permanently in Iroquois country. In 1667 Fathers Frémin, Bruyas and Pierron had come down from Canada, and had surprised the Mohawks by bringing neither destruction nor treachery. The Mohawks, who were forced by the treaty of peace to accept them, could not believe that any army was not following secretly behind them. Once they discovered that the Black Robes came even without any protection, they were somewhat drawn to them. They were even grateful to them. A spirit of companionship indeed grew up between the Mohawks and the Black Robes even on the voyage of the Black Robes to the Mohawk country, for the Black Robes travelled as part of a band of Iroquois, and when the Iroquois were chased by a much larger party of Algonquians — that is the Mohicans, or Loups — the Black Robes were united by a common danger to their escort.

The reception of the Jesuits at Kanawaké was not thus what might have been expected ; it was a real reception. In the first place, the Huron and Algonquian Christians who had been adopted into the Mohawk Nation, now felt for the first time that they could show themselves as Christians. They were jubilant : eager to have Mass celebrated, eager to have their children baptized.

A much stranger thing, however, happened when some Mohawks — I believe they were all women — asked these Jesuits for baptism. When the Jesuits demurred, saying it was too soon, one of these Mohawk women cried out, "At least baptize my son. He is young. He has not my sins."

Among those who asked for baptism, however, Tekakwitha was not one.

After this the Jesuits left Tekakwitha's village and took up various stations among the more important Iroquois villages, but Father Pierron did remain at a village which was Mohawk, their largest one, farther up the Mohawk River. From there he could visit Kanawaké. And we know that he did visit it, and that he baptized a year later the persistent woman who had impressed him on his first visit.

In 1669, he made a very exceptional trip to Kanawaké. Suddenly news came to his village that Kanawaké was being attacked by the same Mohicans whom I mentioned above, and who had grown braver and braver since the French three years back had humbled the Mohawks. Father Pierron accompanied as chaplain the two hundred Mohawk warriors who hastened down the river twenty miles to save Kanawaké. Before they arrived, the village had been saved. The Mohicans had retreated, and the villagers were feasting on one of the Mohicans whom they had captured.

It was too late to do anything about this cannibalism. Father Pierron thought it best to continue on with the two hundred irate Mohawks of the Upper Village whose numbers had been swelled by warriors from Kanawaké, and who were trying to circumvent the retreating Mohicans. They did circumvent them, captured nineteen scalps which they brought home on a pole, and six men-captives and four women-captives, one of the latter of whom had a suckling at her breast,— a babe born in campaign. Father Pierron baptized the suckling before it died. Then he watched the captives— the grown-ones—being made to sing as they marched into Kanawaké. Then he watched them as they were made to perform on the scaffold as Father Isaac Jogues had been made to perform. There was no stopping of these Iroquois ceremonies. All he could do was to instruct as many of the

captives as he could in the Faith and baptize them before
they were burned. In the flames it was possible for a dying
Mohican to recognize Christianity. But the Mohawks triumphant could not catch sight of such a thing. "Look how
the Black-Robe loves our enemies," snarled a Mohawk.
Father Pierron tells us what he answered.

"Thereupon I embraced the opportunity to say to our Ag-
niés that I loved their enemies — but with the same love where-
with JESUS CHRIST loves us all — because, as they had
souls that were immortal, and so capable of being happy in
Heaven, it was part of a Christian's duty to procure the same
happiness for them all; that, besides, we were to form in
Paradise only one beautiful family of true friends, because
there is only one God — Who, loving us all with the same
love, unites in Himself all our hearts; and for that reason
I was under obligation to love their enemies. But, I added,
as for them, besides that common obligation that bound me
to love all men in that wise, I had also a very special love for
them, because JESUS CHRIST, who is the Master of our
lives, had sent me into their country to show them the way
to Heaven, and not into the country of the Loups, their
enemies." *

Some of the Iroquois showed that they were touched by
his words, but Tekakwitha kept her thoughts to herself. It
seems as if her spiritual progress had nothing to do with what
the French and their Black Robes did or did not do during
these years, but rather as if it had to do with what Black
Robes had done in their days of apparent failure; as if the

* Thwaites, vol. LIII, p. 149.

death of Father Isaac Jogues was having its effect on her rather than the life of Father Pierron. And this effect was so far her secret.

Within a year Father Pierron made at Kanawaké an even bolder address. It was on the occasion of a Feast of the Dead held at Tekakwitha's village — the great Iroquois ceremony, the one which took place but every ten years, the one which in spite of its superstition brought tears to the eyes of a Brébeuf. Tekakwitha's father and mother were to be exhumed. They were to be torn up tenderly from a nine-year burial. Some Oneidas had come to the feast, and also various representatives from the great central and most conservative nation of the Onondagas, under their famous sachem — later to become a Christian — Garakontié! The speech of Father Pierron seemed so indiscreet as to be that of a mad-man. He began by analysing mercilessly, after the manner of an Occidental philosopher, the meaning of the Feast of the Dead. What did it all amount to?

The Indians understood his logic, but they could not understand how he could use logic against so holy a thing as their feast. They bade him be silent. But he continued to speak, urging them to give up what they knew to be absurd; which drew upon him the further command to depart. They enforced their command by drowning his unwelcome words in singing. At this, not to be frightened, he appealed to them not as near-Christians but as Iroquois. Had he not by their own code a right to make this speech? And by what Iroquois tradition were they bidding him to depart? They were making, he said, a woman of him, an outsider. If after that,

he did depart, as depart he did, it was only to return with
Garakontié, on whose sense of justice he had called. With
Garakontié's permission and under the protection of that
Onondaga chief, he brought his speech to an end, demanding
of the Indians that as the price of continued friendship with
the French they give up their dreams, their jugglery, their
Feasts of the Dead, and their horrible worship of their war-
god Areskoi.

The consequence of his speech was not such as we should
have expected. The Iroquois gave in. They exchanged
gifts with Father Pierron, and promised to give up their
superstitious rites. How in the world they were willing so to
do is a mystery to us. And how in the world Father Pierron
knew they were ready to make such a concession is a further
mystery. Was it that at all costs they wished to maintain the
French friendship ? I doubt it, for the Iroquois were very
proud, and could, if they had been insulted, throw prudence
to the winds. Was it that they were becoming if not
Christians, at least much more Christian than they cared yet
to acknowledge ? Was it that, though victorious in war, they
were losing confidence in Areskoi ? Father Pierron was
evidently aware that they were ready for some change of
heart, or otherwise he would not have taken so hazardous a
step. The readiness of Garakontié to listen to his words may
have been typical of the other conservative chieftains, who
found the old order crumbling away, and welcomed a new
discipline to restrain drunkenness and irresponsibility. At
any rate here are the words with which Garakontié received
Father Pierron's final counsels : "What he has told thee, and

what he teaches thee are important truths for thy welfare ; they have entered into my heart."

We know what Garakontié said. But Tekakwitha said nothing — not out loud.

The next year something less spectacular but equally extraordinary happened. At New Ossernenon, that is Kanawaké, a Christian chapel rose among the long-houses. It was built by a Jesuit lay-brother, Maigneret, with the help of the Indians. And then beside the chapel came to live a Black Robe, a Jesuit, a Father Boniface, just as if he were parish priest to the village. Unlike Father Pierron, he did not come and go. He remained at Kanawaké. He lived there for the Mohawks of the village, and his chapel stood there for them.

Quite surprisingly the Mohawks flocked to the chapel. Not always did they wish to be made Christians. Not always did they wish to hear Father Boniface expound. One special thing that attracted them was the Christmas crib which Father Boniface erected in the chapel — the first among the Iroquois. He set an image of the Infant Jesus in a cradle, decorated it with boughs of fir and hemlock, and before it set candles. The Indians were ravished at the sight, especially when the sight was made more beautiful by the carols which he taught his converts to sing. It is never really warm at Christmas on the Mohawk, yet on Christmas Day the Mohawks who were not Christians crowded round the chapel, standing all day in the snow, and trying to get a peek at the Infant amid the candles, near to whom Father Boniface on this day, because of the crowding, admitted only the baptized Christians. So infatuated was the village with the Christmas ceremonies that in order to meet its devotion to the mystery of Christmas, Father Boniface "allowed them to continue their Christmas airs and hymns till Easter." *

Tekakwitha may have kneeled in the snow. She did not pluck at the sleeve of Father Boniface nor ask to be admitted nearer.

Very valiant converts began now to appear among the Mohawks. One of these converts who did not hide her conversion under a bushel was Marie Tsiaouentes, a woman; another was the so-called Great Mohawk, Athasata, most famous under his name of Kryn, a man and a chief warrior.

Marie lived not at Kanawaké but at the Middle Castle to the west, but she, like most of the Mohawks to the west, passed through Kanawaké frequently on her eastward visits to the Dutch trading posts. She had been baptized by Father Pierron in the late 1660's, and from a woman conspicuous for her drunkenness in a region where one had to be particularly drunken to be conspicuous for it, she had become a model of sobriety and heroic virtue. What was most remarkable in her, now that she was baptized, was her steadfastness. There was nothing half-hearted about her. When the Dutch bade her throw away her rosary, as being a charm of the Devil's, which would undo her, she defied them with scorn. Similarly she defied those who tried to force brandy on her. Four drunken men on one occasion toppled her over on her back and tried to pour the fire-water they loved between her lips. It was she who conquered, not they.

She was, indeed, a strong woman, a valiant one, and as

* Thwaites, vol. LVII, p. 93.

such, not seeking to be combative. Yet occasions arose on which she seemed to be challenging her comrades. Once on a visit to the Upper Castle she discovered that the feast of which she was partaking was a sorcerer's "eat-all" feast by which somehow a sick woman was to be cured. As soon as Marie discovered the nature of the feast she sprang up. "Whoever is a true Christian, let him follow me, and go out with me. As for those are such only in name, they can remain at this superstitious feast." Four or five women were men enough to follow her.

Marie caused some perturbation among the Mohawks, but nothing like the perturbation that the Great Mohawk, Kryn, caused. His very conversion was a greater surprise than hers. He was, to begin with, the proudest of the Mohawks. He was so proud of being a Mohawk that when the Mohicans dared assault Kanawaké, he felt pierced to the quick of his Mohawk honor. It was he who more than any other beat back the Mohicans. It was he who led the party which pursued the retreating Mohicans and ambushed them, as I have already related. It was he who, still smarting from the Mohican insult, led a Mohawk war-party straightway against the Mohican village farther down on the Hudson, which had a garrison twice the size of his war-party. What if he did fail to storm the village, he did defy it. He did avenge an insult. Such a proud warrior seemed to be the Mohawk of Mohawks. Indeed he was the Mohawk of Mohawks. In him the Mohawks put their trust as in one who could carry on their traditions. His conversion to Christianity was unthinkable.

And it was even more unthinkable because of what had happened to him in his own household. His wife had become converted, and his daughter too, to his disappointment. Then soon after baptism, his daughter had died. He could see in her death only an evidence of the malignity of the Christian faith. He did not behave like a mere obstinate man ; he did not fall into a vengeful rage, but he abandoned his wife. He went off hunting for the winter up by the St. Lawrence River opposite Montreal.

What began his conversion — so far as we can see — was a chance visit that he made on an Indian cabin that he came upon during his winter hunt. He entered this cabin for shelter, and found shelter and more too. He found in the cabin an Indian woman who prayed and ejaculated as she worked. The prayers of this woman impressed him. He began to argue with her. Her answers came back so wisely, so unexpectedly for him, that he remarked : "The one who taught her has a great deal of sense."

Now the one who taught her was a Jesuit, Father Frémin, whom he may have seen visiting Kanawaké in 1667 and who was now founding an Indian Christian settlement at La Prairie (or, in Algonquian, Kentaké or Kentucky) opposite Montreal, and to Father Frémin this Indian woman directed the redoubtable Kryn. Kryn spent the whole winter at La Prairie. All that he had ever dreamed of — he, the fierce Mohawk — he found there. In the early spring he was baptized by Father Frémin. The mere baptism of Kryn was an earthquake at Kanawaké, but what he did when baptized spread even greater consternation in the town. He returned to

Kanawaké, accepted his repudiated wife to be his wife once more, and everywhere in the Mohawk country preached the wonders that he had seen at Kentaké, La Prairie. His enthusiasm was so unfeigned that his eloquence scarcely needed words. His prestige — never lost — gathered his fellow-Mohawks about him, and when he was up and off to go back to La Prairie, and asked how many would like to join him, forty persons responded. One tenth of all the people at Kanawaké trailed after him through the woods.

It is futile to pretend that Tekakwitha, eighteen years old, knew nothing about this. Such a stir did it cause at Kanawaké that Father Bruyas, a missionary even more accredited among the Iroquois than Father Pierron, had to come to the Lower Castle to appease the indignant Mohawks. Father Boniface found it wiser to go North with the exiles than to face the storm of Iroquois wrath. There was nobody in Kanawaké who could be ignorant of such an event. It broke the Mohawk world in two.

Neither is it possible to imagine that Tekakwitha knew nothing about the Black Robes or about the rising tide of Christian faith about her. Her village was a small village, not of isolated New England farm houses of which the inmates could be oblivious to the lives of their nearest neighbors, but of long-houses shoulder to shoulder. They were moreover enclosed by a stockade, which not only served as a protection but also as a symbol that they were a single community. There were at most but four hundred people in her village, and though there were still vestiges of class-distinctions, yet the various classes did not live separately or privately

or speak different languages. Tekakwitha could see the whole
four hundred, and know them, and remark a stranger among
them. She not only saw the Black Robes, and heard the
singing of their church, but she knew their converts, and
knew something of the beliefs of those converts. At least
one woman in her long-house became a Christian. Yet
Tekakwitha neither joined Kryn, nor rallied to those who
were fanatic against him. Kryn did not glance at her twice.
Father Boniface never mentioned her. Neither did Father
Pierron nor Father Bruyas. She was taking her own path,
and her path awakened singularly little interest in others. It
had the appearance of being the most commonplace of paths.

Only one thing during all these momentous years for Kanawaké happened momentous to Tekakwitha. There came
over her a resolution not to marry. It did not take the form
of words. It expressed itself merely in her actions. Mohawk
maidens were betrothed when they were seven, and it can be
presumed that Tekakwitha had so been betrothed. In due
time the man to whom she was betrothed would come to
make the exchange of courtesies which led to marriage.
There was no wooing to be gone through : nothing of our
romanticism. The girl's long-house would have arranged the
affair, taking into account the need of this or that alliance. So
the prospective husband arrived. He offered her a bowl of
hominy. If she partook it, it meant that the marriage would
ensue. She fled away.

CHAPTER VIII

THE BAPTISM OF TEKAKWITHA

IN THE spring of 1675, there came to the Lower Castle, that is Kanawaké, Father Jacques de Lamberville, a Jesuit, thirty-five years old, native of Rouen. As a native of Rouen he had been in a diocese which claimed all of Canada as part of it : also he had a brother who had preceded him to the Iroquois some six years before ; yet, for all of that, he felt very much a foreigner when he arrived at Kanawaké. He had spent in New France already one year during which he had learned a little Iroquois, but his little was very little, and he knew how little it was. He wrote very humbly concerning his ignorance in his letter to Quebec in the following spring. "Although," he said, "I am not very well versed in the language of the Iroquois, with whom I have lived only a year, and consequently cannot labor for their conversion as much as I would like, God has nevertheless had pity on some of the savages who are under my charge."

In the fall of 1675, Father de Lamberville was still so inexperienced at Kanawaké that he made a very important mistake. He entered a long-house which should have been empty, for it was the harvest season, and those who dwelt in it were by right out in the fields. Also it was a long-house which had it not been empty would have been an unwise house to enter, for it contained a household very hostile to the Faith. Father de Lamberville knew neither that it was by rights empty, nor that it was a house to avoid. Neither did he know why he entered it. He did it on the impulse of the moment.

Entering it he discovered that there was a person in it. The person was a girl who knew well why she was there. She had injured her foot during the labors of the previous day and could not walk : she had to be there. But this girl did not know everything. She had during the previous years evaded marriage, yet without knowing why she did it. Some great desire kept her from it. Neither did she know how she could continue to remain unmarried. In times past there had been vestal virgins among the Iroquois. Even till recently they had lasted among the Onondagas, having lately disappeared in shame when some French traders demoralized their lodge with liquor. But among the Mohawks, in their villages, so much smaller than the Onondaga capital, to be a vestal virgin was out of the question. Every Mohawk girl had to marry. Otherwise there was no place for her in the economic and social order. Yet here was this girl, over eighteen and unmarried — a thing unheard of. She did not know whither she was tending, nor why she was where she was. She could not see why her family had been so tolerant with her as not to force her to marry. She was living in a great darkness that covered her even at noonday. Her name was Tekakwitha.

Father de Lamberville, who did not know why he entered this long-house, had come face to face with a girl who did not know why she was acting as she did. He began to speak to her. Before he had spoken to her long, she asked him for baptism.

A half a year later she was led to St. Peter's Chapel at Kanawaké, which Father Boniface had built, and there she was baptized by Father de Lamberville, and called after the famous virgin martyr of Alexandria, Catherine. Immediately she became not merely one of the Christians at Kanawaké: she became "The Christian." As such she was referred to. As such she was acclaimed. Even the pagan Mohawks rejoiced at her baptism, and rejoiced, too, to see her going to her devotions. In a curious way she became the favorite of the village. But not for long.

Very soon the word "Christian" came to be snarled at her: there goes "The Christian." Some people tried to pronounce it as if it was another term for "a lazy person": Catherine would not work either on Sundays, or on the great feast-days. Nobody really thought she was lazy, for her diligence was proverbial, but it was easy for them to pretend that they thought she was lazy. Certainly there was more work for them to do when she was not working in the fields on a Sunday. So they decided to starve the lazy Christian out of her. If she chose to stay behind in the long-house on Sundays, she would find there nothing to eat. Sundays became her fast days. It was no laughing matter.

Next, there was an attempt to make the term Christian synonymous with immoral — which was more difficult. Catherine's aunt, the wife of her uncle, accused her of stepping between her and her husband. And why? Simply because

Catherine — so she said — had once addressed her uncle not as uncle, a name generally given to elders, or to those of a father's generation, but by his name such as a wife only might use.

The mere slip of the tongue was an offense in Iroquois eyes ; there is no doubt about that. If Catherine had really made such a slip she was guilty of a serious breach of Iroquois law. But it is easy to doubt if she made such a slip, for the aunt was obviously not concerned with the slip at all. She ran not to the Mohawk elders, but to the priest, Father de Lamberville, and complained to him of Catherine's impurity. He heard the grounds of suspicion and rebuked the aunt.

Probably nobody at Kanawaké believed the accusations that were brought against Catherine, but that did not help her. She came to be disliked for accusations which were not brought against her, but which were true. Her conduct was a rebuke to the growing impurity and drunkenness of the village. Such a rebuke was resented. Also she was firmer than some Christians in staying away from the Iroquois rites. Catherine had always had a detestation of the cruelties to captives, to the cult of Areskoi. The "eat-all" feasts she had loathed. Now she knew why she loathed such things. She avoided them. All the spleen that the other Christians could avoid by being mediocre fell upon her. She was not allowed to pray in privacy. She was hooted at. She was starved. She suffered for all. She became indeed "The Christian."

Curiously enough the pagan Mohawk who treated Catherine best seems to have been her uncle. He had prohibited neither her instruction in the Christian Faith nor her baptism.

He had been friendly enough with her to take her with him to Fort Orange on that trip during which, so his wife said, Catherine had called him by his real name, not by the title uncle. But this forbearance of her uncle can, I think, be ascribed rather to his sagacity than to his sympathy or sense of justice. He was a chief who knew the dispositions of men, and he knew that Catherine had a will of her own, which opposition only made more her own. Also he feared one thing far more than his village becoming Christian, and that was that its inhabitants should leave it and go to the Christian village opposite Montreal, as Kryn had done. He was willing to choose the lesser of two evils. At all costs the number of people in Kanawaké must not be diminished. Already they were enough hampered in their war against the Mohicans. He preferred to have a Christian, even "The Christian," in his cabin, to having there merely her bed that she had left behind.

The pagan leader had a real intuition in being afraid of the praying village on the Saint Lawrence, for it had a magic in it, not only in attracting Indians from his village, but in prospering beyond human hopes and human plans. It owed its beginning to a Jesuit, Father Raffeix, who did not perceive the consequences of what he was attempting. It had developed, however, in its own manner, in spite of opposition that normally should have crushed it. It was one of those few seeds which could not be kept from growing.

Its history was this : Father Raffeix had, in the year 1667, taken charge of a tract of land opposite Montreal, four miles in its frontage of the St. Lawrence River, twelve miles in

depth. This tract did not belong to him, personally; it belonged to his order, the Jesuits. It had been given to the
Jesuits twenty years before by de Lauzon, at the solicitation
of the Jesuits. Why the Jesuits had solicited such a gift is
well known. They had always dread lest New France continued to be a mere trading-post for the fur-dealers. From the
first they had pleaded for colonists who would settle on
the land, till it, and become self-sufficing. They believed that
these colonists could help in the task of converting the Indians,
and that they were necessary for the defence and maintenance
of New France, as indeed they were, and as ultimately the
lack of them was to prove. The Jesuits accordingly had asked
for the land as a "seigneurie" in order that they might show
on it how farmers could be planted on the shores of the St.
Lawrence. And for that purpose the grant had been awarded
to them. At the time of the deed of gift, however, it was
impossible for the Jesuits to take advantage of it, for the
Iroquois made the open fields uninhabitable. It was not until
after de Tracy's expedition that the fields were so safe that
Father Raffeix could dare attempt his enterprise. In 1667,
he led a small group of settlers out from behind the stockades
of the various forts: Montreal, Three Rivers, Quebec. It was
a time when the future smiled, when the very fields seemed
paradisiacal. One-third of de Tracy's regiment chose to settle
on them.

Father Raffeix built a little chapel for his agriculturalists.
Around him sprang up a community called La Prairie, which
was both a colony and a mission: the Mission of St. Francis
Xavier. He hoped to attract a few stray Indians to this Mis-

sion and convert them. It would be most helpful if he could get some Iroquois from New York State to settle there, as Father Le Jeune had drawn the Algonquians to Sillery and Three Rivers. Nevertheless his main hopes were with the French.

It was not Father Raffeix's expectations, then, that made La Prairie an Indian settlement. It was rather the action of the Indians themselves, of the Iroquois, and particularly the action of a prominent one among them, an Oneida, Francis Tonsahoten, which gave the place its Indian destiny. Francis Tonsahoten began this destiny by establishing himself, his wife, and five of his fellow Oneidas in the vicinity of the chapel almost as soon as it was built.

It is very strange how an Oneida came to do this, and the story takes us back to the days of Huronia which place Francis had visited, probably as a captive, and where he had been taught the "prayer" of Christians and had been baptized. Then there came twenty years during which Francis Tonsahoten lived among his Oneidas, segregated from any Christian influence, hiding his Christian allegiance deep in his heart. Probably the only mention he ever made of Christian doctrines during nearly twenty years was to his wife, a wonderful woman, a captive from the Erie Nation, Gandeakena. His wife used to ask him to explain things, and in explaining the Christian mysteries he reminded himself of them.

Then came Father Bruyas to the Oneida Castle. Francis entertained the Jesuit, and befriended him. This was welcome, but not entirely strange, for Francis had not lost his

Faith. It was strange, however, how Francis's wife, Gandea-kena, helped him, for she was not as yet a Christian. It was she who aided Father Bruyas to instruct and baptize her husband's aunt. She was even more hospitable than her husband.

In the late summer of 1667, Francis started in a party of eight to visit the French settlements in Canada. He had several motives. His friend, Father Bruyas, had asked him to escort a Jesuit "donné," Charles Boquet, back to Montreal. Also he had need of medicaments for a sore foot, which medicaments Father Bruyas may have hinted he could get from the Hospital Sisters. Possibly he may have had a half-conscious desire to show his wife, who was one of the eight of the party, how the Christian French lived. This party was made up of Francis, his wife, Boquet, and five Oneidas. And they were starting for Montreal just when Father Raffeix was finishing a little chapel at La Prairie, hoping that possibly a stray Indian or two might there worship.

One thing is certain : Tonsahoten knew nothing of the chapel or of the settlement. He merely fell upon it. Once he found it, once he stumbled on a community where he could be really openly a Christian, he began to be conscious of what spiritual privations he had been through. He did not at first join the Community. He merely passed the winter in it, learning during that winter much about the Faith.

Spring came. It must have been at Father Raffeix's sug-gestion that they went not back to the Oneidas, but first — as if merely to see more — to Quebec. At Quebec they saw the holiness of the nuns, who always fascinated the Indians.

They saw the Christian Huron Indians at Lorette whose conduct they could not but contrast with that of the Indians of Oneida, who in these years were becoming very uncompanionable by their drunkenness. An entry in Father Bruyas's diary, an entry of August 16, 1669, may give us an inkling of what the Oneida drunkenness was like :

"The 16th. People return from trading, with sixty kegs of brandy brought from New Holland. A drunken man breaks in the door of my Chapel, reproaching me for the insolence of our Frenchmen. Another strikes my companion, with such violence that he bears the mark of it. Owing to the disorders that are prevailing in this Village, I take occasion to go on a trip toward our Lake, where there are some fishermen — although I am still very weak from a tertian fever which, by the grace of God, has not stopped or hindered me from working for the instruction of my little flock. The heaviest cross that I have is that of the drunkards ; and I have need of all my little virtue to bear it patiently. It breaks up all our exercises, and all our teaching ; and prevents the people from coming to the Chapel to say their prayers, morning and evening — each one thinking only of running away and hiding, in order to avoid the violence of these furious men." *

The sight of White Men, even of Christian — really Christian — White Men, to savages is not always edifying, for there are plenty of faults even in those who approximate to sanctity which can distract one's attention from their virtues. It is greatly to the credit of the inhabitants of Quebec, that after their visit there, five Oneidas, and an adopted Oneida, a

* Thwaites, vol. LIII, p. 241.

woman Gandeakena, had a higher idea of Christians than before, and asked to be baptized. All six of them were baptized by Bishop Laval, while Francis Xavier Tonsahoten knelt in the background.

Francis Tonsahoten cannot be left in the background. He must be praised as being, quite as much as Father Raffeix, the founder of La Prairie, for he now led his party back to La Prairie there to join the settlement which he was to turn into an Indian settlement. And yet if we mention him as a founder we must also mention his wife. It was she who after her baptism begged her husband not to return to the Oneida Castle, but to join the Christians by the St. Lawrence. It was she who after the Oneidas had listened to her plea, and had settled near the chapel of Father Raffeix, attracted more and more hunting Indians to visit there, so that before three years were out twenty Indian families — most of them Iroquois — had settled there.

Owing to the arrival of the Oneidas the destiny of La Prairie became entirely changed. It was a place for the Indians rather than for the White Men. In fact the French became rather a hindrance to the settlement than a help. Not that they quarrelled with the Indians. At first in the small chapel the French worshipped on one side, the Indians on the other. Then when there were too many Indians they attended Mass at different hours, but continued their amity. The trouble came through the desire of some of the French to make money out of the Indians. One Frenchman set up a dram-shop in La Prairie. At this time there was no law in New France which could prevent this, for the Council, being disturbed lest the fur-trade pass to the English at Hudson's Bay or to the English and Dutch on the Hudson River, had tried to salve their consciences and save their trade by making a law that liquor could be sold to the savages everywhere, but not enough to make them drunk. For a time the excommunication of Bishop Laval against those who sold liquor to the Indians was the only sanction against the indiscriminate filling of the Indians with brandy. But nevertheless Father Frémin, who had succeeded Father Raffeix, appealed to the Governor, Frontenac ; and the Governor who was indebted to Father Frémin for having succored a starving fort of his, did, in spite of his over-solicitude for the well-being of the fur-trade, close the shop.

This did not entirely mend affairs, however, for across the river Montreal was turning from a holy city into a fur-mart. Twice a year it held its fairs, which were so bacchanalian that the echo of them brought the Ottawa Indians, with ever-increasing eagerness, fur-laden from Lake Michigan. The noise, the debauchery, which lured Ottawas from so far, could not help but exercise its fascination over the Indians of La Prairie who could see the hilarities from across the river. The missionaries came to the conclusion that the Indian settlement ought to be moved farther from Montreal.

At this crisis, the Intendant of New France, Duchesneau, stepped in and presented Father Frémin with a tract of land farther up the river. It was three or four miles from where there had been once a dram-shop at La Prairie. It was round a bend in the river, so that Montreal, although it could always be reached, could not be seen. It had the advantage of possessing a more fertile soil than La Prairie. It took its name quite naturally from the Sault St. Louis Rapids which made the huge St. Lawrence boil in front of it. It called itself therefore one of the many versions of the title *At the Falls,* or in Iroquois, Kanawaka. The Indians therefore moved to Kanawaka, or as this Kanawaka is spelled, Caughnawaga, and quite unconsciously set up a village which even in name became the Christian counterpart of the pagan Kanawaké on the Mohawk.

From now on the French regarded it as what it was : an Indian town, though Christian. The civil and military authorities did not, in general, like it as such. In 1672 there had come to New France the famous and picturesque governor, Frontenac. He had many qualities which made him an excellent governor, but he was by temperament overbearing, and anybody who stood in his way was not only in the way but also in the wrong. The great task ahead of him was to maintain New France, and it was no easy one, for though King Louis had in 1665 sent over the invaluable regiment which brought peace with the Iroquois, the same King was now engaged in his Dutch war. He could take little direct interest in New France.

Financially Frontenac had to shift for himself. Shifting for himself meant stimulating at all costs the fur-trade, which was languishing because of English and Dutch competition. It meant that liquor would have to be sold to the Indians. Otherwise the Indians would go to the Dutch. Otherwise New France would starve. Otherwise there would be no New France. The Bishop of Quebec, Laval, the priests in general, and especially the Jesuits * tried to prevent the sale of liquor to the Indians, and by so doing proved themselves, to Frontenac's eyes, impractical. Impractical in regard to immediate financial returns they certainly were, and Frontenac had a right to so call them. But because they were against him, they were not only impractical, they were everything that was bad : they were greedy, they were after power, they were wicked. It was only in fits of temper that he stormed thus. He knew very well in his heart that New France could not continue without the priests, but even in his friendly moments he was bent on keeping the clergy and missionaries as much under his control as possible. He was opposed to anything that resembled an autonomous community of Indians controlled by Jesuits. He and the practical men who had to run New France looked askance at Caughnawaga. Frontenac wrote to the King in order to have the deed of gift which gave the Jesuits their new land, The Sault, cancelled. Frémin wrote also to France with his side of the story.

A wonderful letter came back : most kingly. It never mentioned the quarrel between Frontenac and the Jesuits. It agreed with both sides, and then calmly confirmed the deed of gift. Louis XIV saved the mission.

But if the new Kanawaké made some of the Frenchmen

---

* The Jesuit Dablon wrote very strongly in 1673 (Thwaites, vol. LVIII, p. 83) : "Brandy has ruined the Algonquian missions and it still prevents many savages from being converted. The insatiable avarice of the French is the cause of it. They go as far as two and three hundred leagues to seek the savages in the woods for the purpose of getting furs by making them intoxicated." The Relations ceased in 1673.

indignant, it made all the Christian Indians jubilant. They recognized it as an Indian place, where they could be Christians without ceasing to be Indians. Ever since the refoundation of New France in 1632, there had been a slight tug between those who wished to turn them into Christian Frenchmen, and those who wished to turn them into Christian Indians, between the royal government and the Jesuits. Cardinal Richelieu had expressed the attitude of the Royal Government when in 1633 he had offered French citizenship to every Indian convert. Thirty-four years later Talon, the able Intendant of the colony, showed that the attitude still persisted when he wrote to Colbert: "The Jesuit Fathers, to whom I have made a kind of a reproach, though civilly enough, of not having up to now given the attention, they should, to the polishing of the natures of the savages and to the cultivation of their manners, have promised me that they would work to change the barbarians in every respect, beginning by their language." * Already in compliance with the royal will the Jesuits had done what they could do to change the savages in every respect — they had tried to transform Huron boys into French boys at Quebec with no success whatsoever — and they were still willing not to be obstinate against the plans inherited from Richelieu; but they had grown perfectly well aware that, as an Algonquin had once said, an Indian could not be turned into a Frenchman unless he exchanged skins with the Frenchman, and that as Marie de L'Incarnation had said: "A Frenchman can more easily become a savage than a savage a Frenchman." † Therefore they

* Rochemonteix, vol. 1, p. 292.   † *Ibid.*, p. 293.

were forced to take up a position of respect for the Indian-as-
an-Indian which the royal officials did not partake, and which
the latter more and more resented. Frontenac in particular
resented it. To be protected from aggressive and impossible
"francization" the Indians looked more and more to the
Jesuits as their friends. When the land by the Sault, Caughnawaga, was thus definitely awarded to the Jesuits, the Indians
took it as their victory.

In accordance with Jesuit policy the Iroquois at the new
mission were encouraged to develop what was best in their
own traditions. They were allowed to govern themselves.
At first they had one civil chief, and one religious one. Then,
as the community grew still larger, there came a kind of representation by tribes. There were three chiefs, a Huron, an
Onondaga and a Mohawk. Once there was a quarrel and a
schism. The Hurons moved across the St. Lawrence to another mission settlement conducted by the Sulpicians, north
of Montreal. But, on the whole, the unity at the new Caughnawaga was remarkable, and even the Hurons who had left
them bore them no animosity. The Hurons of Lorette near
Quebec sent them, as a pledge of their friendship, a strip of
wampum which can be seen at Caughnawaga to this day.
Caughnawaga became a place where Indians lived — there were
representatives of twenty tribes among them — and where they
ruled and where they kept the peace. The only White Men
among them were the priests. The priest in charge was
Father Frémin who was indubitably a Frenchman, and yet
who had lived in every village of their Five Nations. He
knew the Iroquois Long-house from the Mohawk to the

Genesee River. He knew their tongues. He was their priest.

Caughnawaga became not only a truly Indian place, but a
Christian Indian place. It had a chapel sixty feet long. There
was a bell in the chapel from which rang the Angelus three
times a day. Drunkenness was discouraged by the homeliest
of methods. The drunkard was thrown in the pig-pen to
rest there for a day. It was even more thoroughly repressed
by public opinion. A very happy spirit animated the community. The Indians, Algonquian or Iroquois, had never
complained of physical hardship. They had borne it stoically.
They had also been marvelously hospitable. Now their patience and hospitality were raised to a higher, more cheerful
degree. There were, in the spring of 1676 when the Indians
moved from La Prairie to the Sault, two hundred Indians
permanently in the community. During that year they gave
hospitality to three hundred visitors, whom they had to feed
for longer or shorter periods. This was hospitality on an unprecedented scale. It was charity. In order to practice it
they had to work harder in the fields than it had ever been
their habit in the Iroquois — not to mention the Algonquian —
settlements. They did it willingly.

Yes, they were Indians and Christians, and there was a
battle between their old traditions and the truth. They could
accept the Christian prayer, yet how they clung to what was
dearest to them, their loyalty to the old burial rites ! It was
Gandeakena who put an end to the old customs. She, who
with the name of Catherine, had become the third founder of
La Prairie, and the leader of the whole community in religious

zeal and hospitality to all for the sake of Christ, died in the spring of 1677—a year after she had entered the promised land at Caughnawaga. At her burial no Indian riches were poured into her grave by her husband, nor by those many who loved her. Francis Tonsahoten would have no shadow of pagan superstition at the putting into the earth of the body of one who had ended by teaching him what it was to be a Christian. In her burial only such ceremonies as she would have loved were allowed. Her burial became a precedent for future Christian burials at the mission. Thus in her very death Catherine sealed paganism's end. Caughnawaga, largely through her, had been able to cast off the old darkness. It was beginning to shine.

And with what a light it shone ! Catherine's uncle could not see the light, but he knew it was there. One young Mohawk woman of his own long-house had already gone there with her husband. Kryn had gone there. Hunters from his own village and with his own prejudices had gone there to mock and yet had stayed there. Thinking that one reason why it shone might be its goodly supply of provisions — which to him may have seemed goodly, though to missionaries it seemed paltry almost to starvation — he even sent warriors as guests to the Sault to devour their supplies. But even this visitation had no disastrous effect on the supplies, and it had a very disastrous effect on the guests. Many of them remained with those they had come to rob. Catherine's uncle saw that he could not put out the light. He tried to keep Catherine from looking at it.

Truly it was impossible for her not to look at it. Even if she loved deeply her native village, its soil even (which the half-migratory Iroquois never loved as the Christian peasant does), even if she loved and cherished her own village, she could not help seeing that its best inhabitants had fled, and that those who stayed were degenerating daily. Drunkenness was what mainly degraded them. De Lamberville wrote to Canada that except for brandy he could convert all of Kana-waké. But the brandy was there. Here is another description of what was going on along the Mohawk River at this time.

"One may witness, for many days in succession, all-prevailing drunkenness in the villages ; that means that the greater number of men, being drunk, behave like madmen, and run about everywhere through the streets and into the cabins, as if possessed. They commit at these times a thousand insolent actions ; they fight and actually tear one another with their teeth. One can see wounded men, dead men, and children cast into the fire. And when the women take upon themselves to get drunk — as is often the case ; for they even bring up their children in this vice, taking pleasure in leading through the streets in triumph a young boy or girl, ten or eleven years of age, completely drunk — when, I say, the women as well as the men take part in it, it can be imagined what confusion and disorder that produces. A poor missionary is compelled to remain hidden in his chapel for several days, without daring to come out. Nor is he left even there in quiet ; for often the drunkards try to enter, sometimes breaking in the doors and windows. Very often, the father, surprised in the streets by these infuriated men, has to take to flight ; and, if he do not run faster than they, he may very well fear to be very badly treated by them." *

Possibly Catherine's uncle decided that he could not expect her to like this degenerating Kanawaké. There was nothing left to do, then, except to force her to stay, whether she liked it or not. He sought to intimidate her. He allowed a young Indian to pretend that he had gone mad, and had therefore the shamanistic privileges of a mad-man. The Indian entered Catherine's long-house, and with a directness that showed no madness threatened her with a hatchet, "Cease to be a Christian or die." Catherine was not in the least disturbed. And she did not die.

She went on waiting for an opportunity to escape to Caughnawaga. She was ready to go, and her priest, Father Lamberville had counselled it. Christian life at Kanawaké was so nearly impossible. But the road to the place of prayer was two hundred and fifty miles long. And who could lead her on it ? And how could she evade her uncle ?

Shortly after this, on July 14th, 1677, there arrived on the Mohawk three Christian Indians from Caughnawaga, who came as missionaries to their brethren. They visited the Upper Castle of the Mohawks and there so delighted Father Bruyas that he wrote rapturously of them to Father Frémin.

"Your three good Christians," he says, "came here on the feast of Saint Bonaventure. I may say that God sent them to us at the very moment when they were needed to find those

* Thwaites, vol. LXI, p. 161.

who accompany them on their return; for some of the latter
would have gone to the war had they delayed their arrival
eight days. Oh, what good Christians your two dogiques
are! They completely changed the aspect of our little Church
during the short time that they spent here. Not content with
going into the cabins in the daytime to preach Jesus Christ
crucified, they also devoted a considerable portion of the night
to the same object. Kinnouskouen, that fervent preacher,
gathered our Christians together in the evening—being unable to do so in the daytime, owing to the work in the fields
—and spent two or three hours of the night in instructing
them, and teaching them to sing. One man such as he would
do more good than ten missionaries such as I. I would
greatly desire for the consolation and advancement of this
Church that we should frequently have similar visits. I en-
deavored to show them every possible attention, considering
our state of poverty. Oh, how holy, how blessed is the Mission
that possesses such holy Christians; and how much holier
still is the missionary who has formed them by his care and
toil? *Crescat in mille millia."* *

The Indian praised in this letter as Kinnouskouen (or
catechist) was an Oneida convert who among the Mohawks
still went by his old pagan name Hot Powder. With him
from Canada had come a Christian Huron and a Christian
Mohawk, the latter of whom is generally referred to as a
brother-in-law of Catherine Tekakwitha's, for he had married
a girl of her long-house who had been brought up as Cath-

* Thwaites, vol. LXI, p. 65.

erine's sister. With that sister he had fled to Caughnawaga. These three Indian converts after their visit to the Upper Castle of the Mohawks passed through Catherine's village, known as the Lower Castle, and discovered that Catherine's uncle was away signing a treaty with the Dutch at Fort Orange. It was not an opportunity to be missed. Hot Powder had to continue on to the Oneidas, westward ; but he gave his place in the canoe to Catherine Tekakwitha and sent her northward with the Huron and her brother-in-law.

Twice they were almost intercepted. Catherine's brother-in-law had to buy some provisions from the nearest Dutch settlement, Fort Orange, now Albany. He left Catherine and the Huron in the forest and started off alone in his canoe. Suddenly he found himself face to face with Catherine's uncle, who was returning from having signed the treaty. For some reason the uncle did not recognize him.

As soon as the uncle had returned to Kanawaké he discovered that Catherine had fled. He guessed that some of Hot Powder's catechists had stolen her away from him, and was off to the St. Lawrence. He hurried after them.

Finally, following the regular Iroquois trail up toward Lake Champlain he came upon an Indian who just as he came in sight of him shot an arquebus at the tree-tops and darted off into the forest. He did not know that at the sound of the arquebus his niece, Catherine, walking ahead, had dodged from the path into the thicket. All that he found when he proceeded further on his path was a Huron Indian sitting on a log smoking his pipe. He did not know the Huron. He did not know that all this procedure had been carefully planned to fool him. He decided he was on a false scent and returned home.

Catherine continued. She crossed a lake — two lakes — and then in a canoe floated down the famous river of the Iroquois, the Richelieu. She followed it from where the pagan Iroquois lived to where the Christian Iroquois lived. She left behind her Kanawaké! She came to Caughnawaga.

CHAPTER IX

TEKAKWITHA AT CAUGHNAWAGA

WHEN CATHERINE arrived at Caughnawaga she was received
by two priests who greeted her much as Dante was greeted
by the angel who touched his forehead as he crossed the
threshold of the mountain of purgation. It will be remembered that the angel was kind and ready to let him in, but
that it wrote upon his forehead seven P's, which stood for
the seven sins he was to clear himself from as he gradually
ascended. Similarly the two priests, Fathers Cholenec and
Chauchetière, the former of whom had taken charge of the
mission in the temporary absence of Father Frémin, treated
the fugitive graciously, yet admitted her only as one who
would have a long ascent to make before she would be able
to attain to the level of the Christians at Caughnawaga.

It was true that Catherine brought with her a letter from
Father de Lamberville which ran as follows : "Catherine
Tegakouita is going to live at the Sault. I beg of you, be so
kind as to take her under your direction. You will soon
know the treasure we are giving you. So guard it well. In
your hands it will be for God's glory, and the salvation of a
soul that is assuredly very dear to Him." But letters of
introduction have from the beginning of the world been mere
letters of introduction. Catherine was visibly no different

from any other half-cannibal Iroquois woman, except that she had a hood pulled farther over her head than was customary.

Also these two Fathers were convinced that Father de Lamberville could not possibly have any conception of what a holy Christian life was being practiced at Caughnawaga. They themselves could scarcely believe their own eyes. It was to be expected that he over-rated the sanctity of this Catherine whom he had sent to them, for he had no high standard to judge her by.

Two years before this, when Father Cholenec had just arrived at Caughnawaga, he wrote to France an account of the spirituality of the place. He said that there were three classes of Indians there : the first class composed of catechumens preparing for baptism ; the second class of those who had been baptized, were as yet untested ; the third class of those who were perfecting themselves. His praise of the third and highest class was very high.

"I will say," he writes, "that the Savages of this third class live like perfect Christians, who know how to war against their appetites, and to tame their passions by application and reflection ; who pass whole days without committing a venial sin maliciously or deliberately ; and who without waiting for Sundays or for the nearest festivals, come and confess themselves at all times on the slightest scruple of conscience. Finally they are Christians who detest sin, not only in themselves, but also in others." * And then he went on : "It is true that during the short experience that I have had (he was only thirty-seven), I have seen Frenchmen who made a special

* Thwaites, vol. LXI, p. 61.

vocation of virtue ; but nevertheless with the exception of the secular and regular communities, I admit that I have never seen anything approaching what I have the happiness of witnessing every day ; and, for my own part, I find more pleasure among them in a single day than among the French in many months.   O ! how great a difference there is also !" *

But the most significant clue of all to the high esteem which Father Cholenec had for all the classes at Caughnawaga lies in the compliment he paid to its second class, its middle class spiritually.   He included in it Hot Powder.

Hot Powder, it will be remembered, was the Indian who led down from Caughnawaga the party which ultimately rescued Tekakwitha.   But Hot Powder, as his name suggests, had done other more extraordinary things.   Once upon a time his brother had been killed, and making up his mind that the French had killed him he had dashed off without a second thought to kill some of the French.   But second thoughts came.   In them he was honest enough to see that without a doubt it was not the French who had killed his brother. Pretty surely it was the Algonquins.   But now that he had thought twice, he thought a third time.   To avenge himself on the Algonquins would be to plunge his people into war. It was no light matter.   He had a Christian wife, whose words gave him an even deeper sense of his responsibility. Yet how could he go home to the Oneidas without having man-like avenged his brother's killing ?   In his dilemma he decided to go to Caughnawaga.   There he learned more about the Faith of Christians, asked for baptism and was baptized.

* *Ibid.*, p. 293.

From then on Hot Powder's name was Louis, yet he was still referred to as Hot Powder, for he continued to be as explosive as powder, though now with a Christian motive. He was all vehemence. He minced nothing. It was he who invented the punishment for drunkards at Caughnawaga : the throwing of them to the pigs. He had his own manner of doing things. Indians at the Sault, almost all of them, wore rosaries somehow, somewhere, and very visibly, for they had no pockets to hide them in, no wallets to leave them behind in. But Hot Powder capped it all by wearing his rosary wound fantastically round the crown of his head. He tied it to his scalp lock. He had a great frankness and an irresistible eloquence, filled with metaphors which the poet in him coined without effort. There was nothing mediocre in Hot Powder's zeal, nor mediocre in his perseverance. Yet Father Cholenec put Hot Powder only in the second class.

With such a second class, with such a third class, under their eyes, Fathers Cholenec and Chauchetière could scarcely regard Catherine as a treasure brought to Caughnawaga. It was Caughnawaga that was offering to her a treasure. In order to educate her to the standards of their mission, they put her under the charge of a widow named Anastasie. Even if he had not put her in Anastasie's charge, I suspect that Anastasie would have taken charge of her, for Anastasie lived in the long-house into which Catherine inevitably went : the long-house of her adopted sister. Also Anastasie had known Catherine when she was a child, when she was still Tekakwitha. She had even known Catherine's mother. She had lived in the same long-house as Catherine, both at Ossernenon, and at Kanawaké. She had known Catherine's uncle. She knew more about Catherine than Catherine knew about herself. Catherine was to her still a child, almost her own child, almost her private property.

There is no way of knowing when Anastasie became a Christian. There are no archives in which to look up such details. From the way she talked in later years about the infant Tekakwitha and about Tekakwitha's mother, it would seem, as if she had been a Christian at the time of Tekakwitha's birth. If so, she had been a captive taken from the Hurons or Algonquins, and was presumably furtive in her Christian customs. At any rate after having married, and having brought up a family, and buried a husband, she had turned up at the mission on the St. Lawrence and devoted herself with all her heart to a life of penance and reparation. As a follower of Catherine Gandeakena, she, with that earlier Catherine, had become a member of the Confraternity of the Holy Family which set the Christian example at Caughnawaga. Now that a new Catherine had come to the St. Lawrence she wished to hand on to her the teachings that she had received from the first Catherine.

Here is how she began : "Catherine, do you not wish to be like our Blessed Mother, the Mother of God ? If you do, take from your hair those vain ornaments of wampum." The Iroquois maidens had their pretty vanities as well as other maidens. Above all they liked to decorate their hair, to sleek it with oil till it was raven black and glistening. It was a common decency to adorn it, once it was sleeked, with wampum ornaments. We can hardly imagine that Catherine did not delight in so adorning herself, for she did the adorning. We know also that she was extremely skilful in decorating moccasins with wampum, which she could hardly have been had she lacked an eye for patterns. But quick as a flash and forever she took off her ornaments. Anastasie was hard to please, yet she won Anastasie's admiration.

She also began to win the admiration of the priests. There were two Masses a day at Caughnawaga : one at dawn, one immediately after dawn for the Indians. Catherine could not be kept from attending the two Masses. It was evident, too, that when the Angelus rang its thrice daily, Catherine kneeled each time as if with a real joy. She joined eagerly in all the devotions. She was the most zealous person among the zealous.

If this zeal of hers had been mere youthful enthusiasm, it might have pleased the Jesuits but nothing more. As it was, it impressed them, for it had certain marks to it, which tended to show that it was more than laudable ambition. It was holiness. In the first place it was seen that she was not merely trying to show off to herself. She was thinking of God. This was visible in her attentive, humble fulfilment of all her daily humdrum duties and in her avoidance of any spectacular devotions. In comparison with Kanawaké, Caughnawaga was a very industrious place. Yet though coming from Caughnawaga, Catherine was more industrious than anybody else. There was something in this girl which Anastasie had not taught her.

Next, Father Cholenec, her confessor, began to perceive that she had extraordinary gifts of prayer. He knew that she spent a long time at prayer, but he could not at first be sure that she was not merely kneeling. Little by little through conversation he discovered what went on in her head. This was her procedure : As soon as she entered the chapel in the early morning, she put herself in mind of how wonderful it was to be baptized. She thanked God for baptism. Then she pulled the blanket hood lower over her eyes and bethought herself that Christ was present in the Sacrament of the Altar. She would end her prayers by begging God to have mercy on her kin, on her uncle, on Kanawaké.

It was a further delight to Father Cholenec to find that Catherine was never brooding over herself. It was not of herself that she liked to talk, but of Our Lady. It was to please Our Lady that she had taken so gladly the trinkets from her hair. Long since, like all the convert Iroquois, she had carried a rosary and told her beads. Now she added to her night prayers the Litany of Loretto.

It was from her upward glance at the Blessed Virgin, that without an effort on her part, there seemed to descend upon her and reflect itself from her, the purity which more than anything else delighted Father Cholenec into astonishment.

Having decided that Catherine was no mere beginner, Father Cholenec made a further decision : he would let her receive Holy Communion at this coming Christmas.

To us this may not sound like a momentous decision : we live in the heyday of frequent Communion. At the Sault in 1677 it was an unprecedented step. The more stable Indians at the Mission, those who belonged to the Confraternity of the Holy Family, and others, were, of course, admitted to Holy

Communion as a privilege and as a reward ; but there were many Indians, also pious, who attended the same chapel, yet were made to wait. And certainly no Indian who had been baptized less than two years had been accorded the privilege, and much less one that had been at the Sault for less than half a year. Never in any one of the half dozen chapels in the lands of the Five Nations had Holy Communion ever been offered to the Indians. "Pain bénit," the blessed bread — still distributed in France and in Canada — was there given to the worshippers as a sacramental, the use of which, practiced with reverence, could finally lead up to the reception of the Sacrament of Sacraments.

It is easy to see why there was this reluctance to admit the Iroquois to Holy Communion. It was known that they had certain gross and perverted ideas in their heads, into the terms of which they might translate the Christian doctrine. It cannot be forgotten that Indians from Ossernenon had cut off slices of Jogues's flesh while Jogues was still alive, and had devoured them. They were Mohawks who had eaten the heart of Brébeuf after it had been torn from his mutilated body, while he hung from the stump of a tree in burned St. Ignace. More recently Father Bruyas had discovered his Oneidas roasting slowly to death a woman of the Andastes, a people of their own stock, with whom they had been engaged in an annihilating war. Such tales make us dizzy with sickness. It did seem — did it not ? — that the thoughts of the Iroquois had become so tarnished, and their lips so polluted, that a long purification of lips and thoughts would have to take place before they could see the doctrine of the Blessed

Eucharist, as a child without preconceptions may see it.

Yet even then it must be acknowledged that the Iroquois had been longing very particularly for Holy Communion. The very mirages they had followed showed them famished for it. They had always tried to raise themselves higher than they were by joining themselves somehow to sufferings. And here were the sufferings of Christ with which they could unite themselves. Also the Iroquois had been tormented with the desire of girding themselves into a single body, which was greater than the sum of them all as individuals. In all their wars they had, like most imperialists, fought for an ultimate peace to be enjoyed in the unity of a long-house which was The Long-House.

The union with God, and with the splendor of the saints, and with the heroisms and weaknesses of the Church Militant, made possible by the Sacrament of the Holy Eucharist, was the very thing for which all their wars had been fought, and all their dreams had been dreamed.

When Catherine Tekakwitha approached the rude rail in front of the altar of St. Francis Xavier's Church on Christmas Day, 1677, she was not merely a unique and pure Iroquois girl, who had been baptized a Christian and by God's grace had become worthy of the highest Christian privilege, but she was Catherine who was fulfilling at last the destiny of her race. She stood for all the generations who had so carefully been buried and reburied and commemorated. To have her arrive where she now was was a consummation of their struggles and suffering.

And now there came a bustle in the settlement as if all the

Indians were going to make a trek, as if they were off for a third Caughnawaga. It was the time when the hunting parties set forth. To one of these parties Catherine was attached.

Catherine did not join this party from any private wish of her own. She would have preferred, had there been an alternative offered her, to have stayed at home. There were two reasons why she had an aversion to going forth for two months on a hunting party. One of the reasons we might guess : she would have to be away from the Blessed Sacrament. There would be no Mass in the woods, no priest. The other reason we would not guess : life was too easy in the woods. It was luxurious. Many of the Iroquois restraints were not practised in the woods.

Had the Iroquois villages been like our cities, with heated houses, with lights that defeat and replace the stars, with great stores of stuffs and provisions, then the tables might have been turned, especially if in Iroquois villages it had been possible to have as our cities sometimes accord it, an individual privacy. It would have been a hardship to go into the cold, and away from shelter, and the freedom from moral restraint would have been no greater than at home. But, as it was, hunting was a banquet and a vacation : a banquet because moose and elk might be tracked in the snow, overtaken and eaten ; a vacation because the elders were not about. In the old days, the Iroquois on hunting trips had taken up with new wives, or temporary wives. Things not permitted at home were there permitted. The men ruled. In the eyes of Catherine's companions there was no comparison between a winter life on the chase, and a winter life in the village. In the village there was no meat, no adventure, nothing but day after day of tasteless sagamité.

I suspect that from their old reputation Catherine did not like the hunting trips, but her objection to going on them now was not, it would seem, due to their immorality, for such among the Indians at Caughnawaga had come to an end. They were simply luxurious and gluttonous. They were not penitential enough. She had a desire for penance which it is difficult for us to understand if we try to understand it simply by treating our lack of any such desires as something on which to base our understanding. Catherine, then, did not want to go shelterless into the zero weather, hunting moose : it was too easy for her.

Yet she did go. She knew perfectly well that there had to be hunting trips. There were never any beaver near the Iroquois villages : they had all been killed off. In order to conduct a necessary commerce with the French, beaver-skins had to be secured. They were the soundest currency. Also if everybody stayed at home there would be no corn left over in the spring. If everybody had to go that could go, what right had she to stay home ? Besides that, the last thing she wanted to do was to appear singular. She still looked like every other Mohawk. She would continue to do as they did. So she started off. "Good-bye," she said to Anastasie.

It is fortunate that she went. As Father Cholenec has put it, she needed to go once on a hunting trip from Caughnawaga in order by that once to sanctify all hunting trips. She showed how Christian a life one could live on these trips.

Not that her companions had been forgetting their Christianity when away from their Christian chapel. They had adopted a custom of keeping track of the holy days and of the days of fasting by means of knotted strings. They said every day their prayers in common. They even did missionary work : it was an Indian woman praying aloud on a hunting trip who had converted Kryn. There is a missionary story concerning Hot Powder which is also worth telling. Once he had chanced to fall on a band of Indians orgying into drunkenness. They offered him a drink. It would have been surly to have refused it, and might have brought blows upon his sobriety. It was a cold night. The brandy was hot. He accepted the swig, therefore, and then pretended that he was tipsy. He staggered and tipped over the brandy kettle, pouring the brandy into the embers, only to be laughed at for so doing. His missionary work in this case was not preaching, but it exerted some influence on the Indians, at least for one night. They were soberer the next morning. It serves as an example of what was the general influence of the hunters from Caughnawaga while they were in the woods. Also, although these Christian Indians gorged themselves to bursting when they killed their game, yet they practiced no "eat-all" feasting. They were a Christian influence in the woods.

But Catherine had a more heroic Christian influence. She did various secret things. Once she was caught by her sister-in-law walking in the snow without moccasins at a short distance behind the procession. She wished to suffer with Christ of the Crucifix. During the days when she was encamped she would do the nearest thing to hearing Mass. She would, early in the morning, at the hour when Mass was being celebrated at Caughnawaga, retire into a thicket where she had managed to tie two twigs together to make a cross. There she would pray as if she were at the Mission. These early morning absences of hers were absences that would not be noticed, for it was at an hour when the chores were being done : the wood fetched, the water carried. She merely rose a bit earlier for the chores and continued them later. She stole her prayer-time from her breakfast-time. And often times she was glad to miss breakfast entirely, especially on Wednesdays and Saturdays, on which days she chose to fast. If it was noticed that she was not eating, and came to be invited to eat, she would never refuse the invitation. She would visibly eat, but would secretly sprinkle what she ate with ashes to make it less edible.

At about nine o'clock the men would go forth for the day's hunt. This left the women behind with not too much to do. It was the custom of the women at such times to gossip, and they found that the time dragged less if they tore the reputation of this or that acquaintance to pieces. It is an old-fashioned and new-fashioned diversion, and one which the Iroquois had developed from generation to generation. To a person of Catherine's spirituality the true nature of this murderous diversion appeared. It wrenched her from her conversation with Heaven. Therefore she intervened decisively. With the prestige of her simplicity she invited the women to recount to one another the stories of the saints, such as they had heard them from the priests. Especially the stories of the martyrs appealed to her and to the other Iroquois. Also she started the women singing and kept them singing. This was not difficult, for Father Frémin was, like a half a dozen of the most successful of the missionaries in New France, a musician. He had taught them to sing plain-song : they loved to sing. Also Catherine, who was skillful with her needle, worked with it, encouraging the others to do likewise. Their work was not with a European needle on cloth. It was with a quill on leather. Especially she repaired and decorated the moccasins.

By Palm Sunday, Catherine was back at the long-houses by the St. Lawrence. There is no mention of how good the hunting was, but it is certain that she had become no glutton. Neither had she in the forest lost her habit of prayer. On Easter Sunday she once again received Holy Communion. Shortly afterwards she was admitted to the Confraternity of the Holy Family. She began with it to visit the sick, to catechize the uninstructed, to pray for all. She was the only unmarried member of it. But otherwise she was not peculiar. She had been accepted merely as one of the third and highest Christian class at Caughnawaga.

CHAPTER X

TEKAKWITHA'S VOCATION

BUT CATHERINE was not merely one of the highest class at Caughnawaga. She was already higher than that. Danger, therefore, lay ahead, for surely she would awaken misunderstandings, and thus receive the persecutions even from good people which are a part of the God-given discipline which comes on those who follow such a path. Her troubles — happy troubles — began.

Her first persecution came from a calumniator, but not from a calumniator who wished her harm. She was a woman — a wife — who was less vindictive than most wives who believed what she believed, would be.

One night while on the hunt this woman had waited and waited for her husband to return home. In the morning she awakened and saw that her husband lay asleep sprawled not near her couch, but near Catherine's. It is easy for us to see what had happened. The hunter had returned late at night and thrown himself blindly where he thought was his place. The wife of the man could not be so sure of Catherine's purity. A quite different explanation fitted into her busy imagination.

Shortly afterwards something confirmed her suspicions. She heard her husband invite Catherine to help him repair his canoe. Nothing, again, was more natural : Catherine was skillful with her hands, whereas possibly the poor wife was not. But now the wife was sure they were planning a secret meeting.

After the return of the hunting expedition to Caughnawaga, this wife hastened to Father Frémin with her accusation. Father Frémin was the Superior at the Mission, who had been away during the previous year only because he had to protect the rights of the colony against Frontenac. But away he had been, and he did not know Catherine as the other two Fathers did. He knew enough about her to make him distrust the accusation ; but human frailty could be very frail on hunting trips and he called Catherine to him, and told her the charge.

Her very manner cleared her in his eyes. Instead of vehemently protesting her innocence, like one who has been keeping very carefully a good reputation before men, instead of entering into any rigmarole of explanations like one good at making excuses, she very calmly, as if from a region of absolute peace, denied the accusation. That was all.

Catherine was so obviously not a hypocrite, that any whispers which attributed duplicity to her could disturb neither the community, nor Catherine's thoughts. Calumnies that accused her of what was merely vile, were like gnats to be brushed aside. They were too insignificant to be called persecutions. But real trials were ahead, and to surmount them she had need of strength.

In preparation for them a strength was given to her : the strength of companionship.

One day after her second Holy Communion she was standing before the new, more permanent chapel that was being builded for her village, on which the carpenters were dealing their final blows. Catherine was enraptured as she looked at it, and she ejaculated : "I wonder where my place will be in it," by which she meant to ask on which side the women would gather, on which side the men ; for the ancient custom of separating men and women in church was still in force at the Sault.

Her ejaculation was addressed not entirely to the skies. She was conscious that beside her was standing an Indian woman of about her age, whom she did not know. The strange woman answered her question and Catherine went on with her ejaculations.

"God, indeed," she said, "does like chapels of wood in which to dwell, but better He likes to dwell in our souls." And still she continued, "It is equally true that I do not deserve to enter into this chapel here, even though it is made merely of wood, for I have often chased God from my soul, and in my turn I deserve to be driven forth from it with the dogs."

The strange woman looked at Catherine in amazement, for Catherine's words were the words of her own heart, and from that time on she and Catherine became inseparable companions, each of them different from the other in temperament, yet with the same ejaculations.

This new companion whom Catherine was given, replaced Anastasie, but except that she took Anastasie's place, she in no way resembled Anastasie. Anastasie was respectable and elderly. She had a good name everywhere. She was a matriarch. This young woman, whose Christian and pagan names ran Marie Thérèse Tegaiagenta, was one who was spoken of with hushed voices. She had an evil reputation behind her for drunkenness, and though now she seemed to have reformed, and to have become a devout penitent, she was not looked on as one of sound judgment. She was at best in people's eyes an eccentric.

Yet the vicissitudes of Marie Thérèse's life made her a particularly appropriate companion for Catherine, for they had given her an overpowering sense of God's mercy and incited her to give her all to God.

Marie, like Francis Xavier Tonsahoten and Hot Powder, was an Oneida. She had been baptized by Father Bruyas and then had married. But her marriage took place when floods of brandy were pouring in from the Dutch. Both Marie and her husband became demoralized by the fire-water, she a Christian drunkard, he a pagan. She had the Faith still, and was not beyond a wish to reform, and with that wish she had removed some six years before to the Mission when the Mission was at La Prairie. But even at the Mission she could not keep from brandy. She became discouraged, therefore, and drifted here and drifted there.

In the autumn of 1675, she found herself north of the St. Lawrence on the Ottawa River with her husband and a small nephew. The three of them joined a party of pagan Iroquois, three men, three women and three children, on their winter hunt. It was a most ill-starred venture : little snow, no game. Possibly liquor helped make them improvident. At any rate the whole twelve of the party suddenly discovered that they were really starving, not as the Indians are willing to do, but to death.

One day two of the men went off to hunt at a greater distance. They were both hollow-bellied when they went. When a few days later they returned the two were only one. That one was sleek and round-bellied. Where was his companion? He had died, starved, was the answer. But how then was the answerer so plump and so strong? The explanation given was that they had separated and the survivor had found game. But where was the game? Why had he brought none back with him? Surely not a whole moose had been eaten. There was a silence as they sat round their camp-fire in the winter night, looking at a kettle filled with broth of cooked shoe-strings.

The silence was particularly terrible to Marie Thérèse, for her husband was sick. He could not move, and they had to move. Would he still be considered as a living human being? The Iroquois whom she faced — whose number had been so ominously reduced from nine to eight — began to whisper together. Then they whispered to her. She must leave her husband behind. She knew what that meant. He could be killed as the Algonquians sometimes killed their helpless — mercy killings we call it today.

Other things might happen too. She refused to abandon her husband. Let them depart if they wished. She and her nephew stayed with the sick man. The other eight, five grown-ups, three children, slunk away.

Her husband died. She buried him. And then, still starving, she with a wondrous strength shouldered her little nephew and was off in the tracks of the party that had left her. They were returning toward Montreal. In spite of her burden she overtook them. Marie Thérèse was no weakling.

I wonder if they were glad to see her. They knew she was a Christian, and in spite of her bad habits they stood in awe of her. Perhaps, however, they could put their consciences' burden on her. They asked her a question. What did she, as a Christian, think of the plan that they had of killing three of the party : the widow and two children of the Indian who had previously died ? The deaths of these three could save them all. Yes, it could feed them. Marie Thérèse froze with dread. She dared not speak at all. She answered nothing.

But in her heart there rose a terrible fear for her own self, and for her nephew. Much more reason had they for killing her, than for killing the other widow. And not only would she die, but she would go to the next world covered with sins. Everything that she had tried to forget in drunkenness came bursting upon her. And she began to cry out to God. If only she could confess her sins. She vowed to God that if only He would save her now, she would change her life, she would give it all to Him.

Before the month was out five starving Indians staggered into Montreal. Marie Thérèse was among them.

And Marie, now that the danger was passed, did not even then forget her cry to God. She confessed her sins, and into her weakness flowed a tremendous new strength. It was now no more a question with her as to how she could find brandy, but how was it that she could show her gratitude to God.

She had a new even more devouring thirst. She returned for one winter to the Oneidas. Then she came to Caughnawaga, arriving there during the winter when Catherine and the hunting parties were away. And now as the hunting parties were trailing back into this village, she had suddenly heard the ejaculations of her own heart uttered by a young woman who had just returned, and whom she had so unexpectedly encountered.

It was due to Marie Thérèse that Catherine dared to attempt a manner of life even more dedicated to God than that practiced by the Confraternity of the Holy Family. Her holy desires, which she had kept to herself and half repressed in her fear that they were her own special singularities, she could now discuss out loud with another, and she found that the other shared her desires. Thus the two began to act together, to practice austerities together, to pray together. They became a spontaneous religious order, of which the members were but two. Sometimes they crossed the St. Lawrence and took a look at the nuns who lived there: the Hospital Sisters, and the Teaching Sisters of Marguerite Bourgeois. Both Catherine and Marie Thérèse wished that they could be nuns. They asked each other if they might not take vows like the Sisters: if they might not promise never to marry. They did not consider asking to be admitted to either of these two orders. There was no precedent for that, for they were Iroquois. And they did not wish to cease to be Iroquois. They wished to be Iroquois Sisters.

The difficulty before the two women was not how they could animate their love for God, but how they could order it. It was with a questioning glance that they looked at the nuns : how did the nuns know where to begin, and where to end, their penances ? In their perplexity Marie Thérèse introduced Catherine to another Indian woman who, she thought, could help them. This woman, an Iroquois, who now became a third in their companionship, was Marie Skarighions. Her particular value to them was that she knew more than they did about nuns. She had been a Christian for some years, but had lived not at the Sault, which had scarcely begun, but at the Huron settlement near Quebec of Notre Dame de Lorette. While there this other Marie had fallen sick and had been nursed by the Hospital Sisters of Quebec. She could not forget the experience. It was Heaven on earth to her. And she delighted in telling Catherine and Marie Thérèse how the nuns acted, how they dressed, how they ordered their days. Marie Skarighions found herself listened to like an oracle.

As a result of these conversations, the three women decided to live like nuns. That meant, to begin with, that they should have to live together and cloistered from the rest of the village, a thing which truly in the situation was impossible. The social order, the division of the population into long-houses, did not permit it. What they planned to do then was to move out to an island, a very small island, which faced them in the St. Lawrence, the Isle Aux Hérons. It had its symbolic appropriateness. It was neither at Caughnawaga nor at Montreal. It was austere. It was visibly isolated, yet from it they could easily reach the Sault. It was a convent-site, made not by man's hands, but by the Maker of the St.

Lawrence. It was walled by the deep currents. In it they could pray, mortify (all too easily) their appetites, and from it they could come to the Sault to teach the children, as did the nuns of Margaret Bourgeois at Montreal and the Ursulines at Quebec, or they could nurse the sick, as did the wonderful Hospital Sisters of the same two cities.

They went to Father Frémin with their project. He was not a severe rule-of-thumb disciplinarian. He was even a musician. But also he was a man of great shrewdness and firmness. It was he who had moved the mission from La Prairie. It was he who had withstood the formidable Frontenac, and prevented him from trying to turn the Indians into what they could never be, Frenchmen. Frémin had accomplished wonderful things, but he was not a visionary. He began to ask some very pertinent questions.

How was this convent on a barren isle to support itself ? On whose funds ? On whose harvests ? On the harvests of the island where nothing would grow ? And if these three women wanted the seclusion of nuns, was it well to choose an island where there were scarcely trees enough to hide behind ? And if they wished to be separated from the world why did they encamp on the highway of the St. Lawrence, the one great road of Canada, on which passed the worldly world of the fur-traders ? In short, if God had given them such extraordinary graces, why did they not stay in the long-houses where there was so much to be done in bringing the lives of the Indians more and more in accord with the will of God ? Had they completed an apostolic work which was before their very faces ?

Father Frémin even smiled at their earnestness — which must have been painful to those smiled at — but they were not offended. They saw the wisdom in his questions, and gave up an idea which even though it had been proven foolish, was nevertheless their own, the child of their heads, one which petulantly they might have clung to. They gave up for the moment any desire to form a convent. Catherine and Marie Thérèse did say to each other that they each renounced the prospect of marrying. They would live as they were, in the world, yet as much as possible like nuns, unmarried.

While Catherine was thus making plans for herself somewhat tentatively, her long-house was making plans — quite different plans — for her with no such hesitation. The long-house took it for granted that Catherine sooner or later must marry : all Indians married. And all the French too married except those who were priests or nuns. Catherine could become neither a priest nor a nun. There were no two sides to the question. Catherine would have to marry. It is easy to see how the people of Catherine's long-house thought they were doing her a favor in spurring her to marry. We do not have to imagine that they had grown inhospitable, or that they had changed their minds about her sanctity, or that they wished greedily, or providently, to have a new young warrior in their long-house as Catherine's husband to help in the work. The best sense these Indians possessed told them Catherine should, for her good and the general good, marry.

And also various actions of Catherine, which they remarked, made them convinced that now was the time for her to marry.

Shall we mention the actions? She was associating with a
certain Marie Thérèse, who, poor woman, had been partly deranged — so it seemed — by her sufferings several winters ago
in the forests above Montreal. Marie Thérèse was pious, but
she was not such a person as one would choose for a guide,
not when there were such women as Anastasie around.
Catherine had not only begun to associate with Marie Thérèse,
but she was acquiring some of Marie's eccentricity. She
imagined she might live as a nun. Care must be taken that
Catherine did not become a dabbler in dreams, and follow
her madness as the pagans did. Her obstinacy which had
stood her in good stead on the Mohawk, should become disci-
plined on the St. Lawrence. Otherwise it might turn into
wilfulness. Nothing could be sager than for Catherine to
take to herself a good Christian husband, who would surely
cure her of obstinacy by his own obstinacy, and who would
put an end to her day-dreams by the many day-labors which
as his wife she would have to perform.

It was Catherine's adopted sister who first broached the
plans of the long-house to Catherine. She came to Catherine
with compliments and a smile. Was it not time now that
Catherine who had made such progress at the Mission, and
had gained for herself there such a good name, should now
make herself really a part of the place, should marry? The
adopted sister did not mention Marie Thérèse. She was no
such fool as to tell Catherine that she feared she might grow
obstinate. Her reasonings were more general. It was unwise for any Iroquois girl not to marry. She might, if she

did not marry, expose herself to temptations which otherwise she might not have. Was it fair to expose herself to such temptation ? To this homily which was somewhat perfunctory, for I do not believe that she believed that Catherine would succumb to any such temptations, she added another. Catherine would need someone to take care of her, to supply her with food ! Catherine must think of Catherine's health. The reasons she advanced (which were reported to us by Father Cholenec) may sound hypocritical, but the real reasons she had for speaking to Catherine and urging her to marriage were not hypocritical. Genuinely she considered that she was swaying a somewhat obstinate sister into the right path. She was doing it gently.

Catherine answered with words which were in keeping with those which she had just heard. She made no mention of Marie Thérèse, nor of the scheme which she had conceived, only to have it laughed at by Father Frémin ; nor of her secret resolution somehow to avoid marriage. She thanked her sister, said that with God's help she could resist temptations, and easily put up with the hardships of her single life. She would not even be a burden to others, for she had few needs. And then she begged her sister not to bring up the matter of marriage again.

More strong methods would have to be used to bend Catherine's will to marriage. Anastasie, who was a matriarch, offered to talk to Catherine with matriarchical authority. She had twice Catherine's number of years, and she would show Catherine that she had twice her sense. What did Catherine mean by burdening her sister ? Didn't she know that it was

her duty to be married ? And what objection did Catherine
have to marriage ? It was a wonderful thing, marriage.
Catherine did not know about it ; she did.

The last part of Anastasie's speech aroused in Catherine an
asperity that she seldom showed. Perhaps she did not think
Anastasie in praising marriage was really speaking from her
heart. Some falsity in the tone aroused her. She asked
Anastasie, why, if she liked marriage so much, she did not
herself remarry. Anastasie departed ruffled and irate.

But Catherine herself was in great distress. What right did
she really have, herself, to resist marriage ? She went to the
priest, who happened to be Father Cholenec, for Father Frémin had gone this time to France to plead the cause of his
Indian Reserve. Wasn't the state of virginity higher than the
married state ? Yes it was, but what made her think she was
called to it. No, she did not have to marry. She should not
be forced to marry. But she should, none the less, not hur-
riedly resolve not to marry. She should consider a long time
the penury that living single might bring upon her. She
should give long thought too, to the question of the temptations concerning which so much was being said. But how
long should she think it over ? Father Cholenec suggested
that she wait a long time — months.

But already — so she claimed — she had considered the matter a very long time. Well, then, three days. She departed
to think it over for three days.

In fifteen minutes she was back. It was not haste. She
could put up the pretense no longer. Father Cholenec realized
that she had already done the waiting. She had decided not

to marry, and he was so impressed with her directness that he then and there blessed her resolution not to marry. He decided to take her part. He would defend her rights.

And while he was thinking this over, pondering on the unexpected resolution of this Iroquois girl, in came Anastasie. She had not been able to calm herself. Catherine had asked why she did not remarry. Catherine for once had become disobedient. All the kinds of pride that she still had in her were offended and uneasy. But before she had a chance to finish her sentences, Father Cholenec, deeply moved by the piety he had seen in Catherine, interrupted her. He told her she ought to be ashamed of herself to have spoken as she did to Catherine. She knew perfectly well, as a well-instructed Christian, what a glorious state was virginity dedicated to God. And here she was, trying to discourage a disciple of hers from attaining to it. We have his own account of his own words. She should be happy that "God had chosen from her own cabin a girl who should lift aloft among the Indians the banner of virginity, and reveal to their minds the sublime way of life which makes earthly men like to heavenly angels." *

Stung by this rebuke, Anastasie behaved as most people who have been so stung do not behave. She acknowledged her mistake to Father Cholenec, acknowledged it to Catherine. She became the supporter of Catherine in Catherine's unprecedented adventure. In other words Anastasie became, as some may well think, the real heroine of this entire incident. She showed a humility in her discomfiture, which wins

* Cholenec, *Life,* p. 43.

her a place in our hearts which she might not have won if we had known her merely as the older, austere woman who had ordered the trinkets out of Catherine's braided Iroquois hair.

This persecution which Catherine had just endured, and which she was now free from, may not seem to some to have been a persecution at all. Those who like to read of persecution in terms of blood-shed, may think it to have been a tame ordeal. Yet it caused Catherine the real torment of doubt. It came from those she loved, and whose judgment she respected. To have them disagree with her made her distrust the innermost promptings of her heart. It inflicted on her a pain less tolerable to her than the bodily punishment to which her race was used. She was, because of it, in an agony of spirit, torn and twisted by two desires, both seeming good, each opposed to the other. By this persecution she suffered her own invisible rack.

All of which becomes plainly visible in the joy which now emanated from her. She was free. She had found her path. There was no contradiction between what God seemed to be asking of her, and what God through His Church was leading her to do. She had but one obedience. It was a joy of being made whole that began the moment she had received Father Cholenec's approbation of her resolution. It was a liberty which received its seal and confirmation when, in the spring of 1679, on the Feast of the Annunciation, she took what is prudently termed to be the first known vow of perpetual virginity ever taken by any Indian maiden of North America.

Father Cholenec officiated at it, and it was he also who wrote the account of it.

"It was on the day of the Annunciation, the twenty-fifth of March, 1679, at eight o'clock in the morning, that Catherine Tekakwitha a moment after Jesus Christ had been given to her in Holy Communion, gave herself also entirely to Him, and renouncing marriage forever, promised to Him her perpetual virginity, and finally with a heart on fire with love called on Him to deign to be her unique spouse, and to take herself as His spouse in return. She prayed Our Lady that Our Lady might with tender devotion present her to her Divine Son; then wishing to make a double sacrifice in a single act, she at the same time as she gave herself devout to Jesus Christ, consecrated herself wholly to Mary begging her to be from then on her mother, and to take her as her daughter." *

As soon as Catherine had taken this vow, or rather as soon as in the preceding summer she had been allowed to entertain the intention of taking it, she became at Caughnawaga a woman set apart from the others. To be set apart gave her a courage to do some things which had she been more firmly woven into the temporal organization of the place, she might have hesitated to do. For instance, in the winter which immediately preceded her vow, that of 1678-79, she had dared to stay at the Sault instead of conforming and going forth on the winter hunt, a privilege, or if you will an abnegation of hers, which was readily accorded to her by public opinion, for was she not an exception ? Had she not chosen a path higher

* Cholenec, p. 51.

and more difficult than that of any of them ? Catherine began to play at Caughnawaga much the kind of rôle that Madame Acarie had played in Paris.

It is astonishing how the Indians, her companions, accepted her as unique, how they recognized in her something really different. It was no outward strangeness of dress that accentuated her singularity. Her dress was the ordinary Iroquois dress. She had always, perhaps from modesty, perhaps from too great sensitiveness in her eyes, worn her blanket hood pulled lower over her face than was customary, but that had been her custom even back at Kanawaké. She also had changed her red blanket — the favorite Iroquois color — to a blue blanket. Otherwise there was no oddity in her. When she took her vow she offered to cut off her hair, but Father Cholenec dissuaded her. She continued to wear the two braids of the unmarried Iroquois maiden.

If we read her two contemporary biographies, that by Father Cholenec, or that by Father Chauchetière — especially if we read them without reflection — we may come to the wrong conclusion that she established her singularity by her extraordinary penances. She did practice painful austerities. She and Marie Thérèse whipped each other with briars. Once Catherine tried on herself a torment which makes us wince when we read about it. She and Marie Thérèse were discussing what was the greatest pain that could be experienced on this earth. Ominously, from the mouth of an Iroquois, came the word of Marie Thérèse : fire. Before many minutes had passed both Catherine and Marie Thérèse were putting live coals on the sensitive flesh between their toes. Marie Thérèse could not support the pain for an instant, not for half an instant. Catherine — so Marie Thérèse related it later — held the coal in place for one, two, three seconds. She did not seem to be able to wince.

And there are still other stories. Catherine had heard Cholenec telling of how Saint Louis de Gonzaga had slept on thorns. Without consulting Father Cholenec, she tried to imitate Saint Louis de Gonzaga. She strewed her bed for several nights with thorns and slept or lay awake on them. This penace could not easily be hid from those about her. It was noticed, and news of it was brought to Father Cholenec, who instantly forbade Catherine to continue with it.

Other penances of hers gave less sharp pain, but may have left a deeper mark on her, for they were repeated and repeated. It must have tested her perseverance, night after night, in winter, to make a circuit of the village, waist deep in the snow, telling her rosary. Such a penance she clung to.

Catherine's penances cannot be left out of any story of her life, for though it is true that penances do not prove charity, when was it that charity did not mortify itself? They are important as a necessary part of the story of Catherine's love for God. They may not be understood by mathematicians, but they cannot help but be understood by lovers. A lover will prize a relic of her whom he loves. He will wear it with dear folly in order to bring one who is far away near. There is always for those who love Christ a relic of Him ready to be worn : some of the pain that He wore on the Cross. Those who fall in love with Christ, and not merely with what He gives them, always fall also in love with the Cross.

At the same time the extravagance of the penances which
Catherine practiced were not what distinguished her at the
Sault, for the Sault was a place of very extravagant penances.
Bodily mortification was a language of love which the Indians
could well understand. It was accessible to all of them. It
fitted in well with the Iroquois ideals of heroic endurance.
Kryn, the Great Mohawk, was at this time the virtual king
of the Sault. He not only ruled, but he ruled with justice.
He was not a fanatic.

Once when the French, who were ready to believe the
worst of the Indians at the Sault, spread the report that an
Algonquin who had been killed had been killed by Father
Frémin's Indians, Kryn went to the scene of the murder, held
an inquest and proved conclusively that the murderers had
been Mohicans. He was also a masterly man, one who, when
the regulations were made forbidding the inhabitants of
Caughnawaga to go to Montreal during the fur-fairs, enforced
those regulations. Yet Kryn was as simple and direct as a
child in his penances. He forgot dignity and lordliness of
which the Iroquois had a great deal, and on every Friday
wound a chain with sharp points in it round his waist, and
going forth into the woods tied to his chain the largest pile of
faggots he could find. Then he dragged it back to the camp,
straining as a beast of burden might do to it, but rejoicing
like a Christian that for Christ he could feel the sharp pain
which the points of the chain cutting into his flesh gave him.
He was probably the only statesman in the world at that time
so rejoicing.

But the penances of Kryn and of his two friends, Etienne,

and Paul Honoguenhag, the latter of whom was dogique, or prayer-leader, at the Sault — all three of whom acted together in a band as did Catherine, Marie Thérèse and Marie Skarighions — were, if incongruous to our dollar-and-cents eyes, in no wise as excessive as those of the women; for women, as Father Cholenec remarked, are much more inclined to excess than men. One woman at the Sault plunged into the St. Lawrence River three zero nights — zero Farenheit — in succession, and stood neck-deep reciting her rosary. When she returned to her cabin she did not dare to approach the fire lest it be remarked that she was drenched. She hid in her corner armored in her clothing of melting ice. As a result she nearly died of fever, and had to be scolded by the priests.

Another equally well-meaning woman was even more absurd, though fortunately without the consequences of bringing fever on herself or anyone else. She plunged into the winter St. Lawrence at least once carrying with her her three-year child. "Let the child," she said, "perform his penances now instead of later."

Seen against the background of such penances, the penances of Catherine stand not for excess, but for sobriety. In the race to do the hardest thing simply because it was hardest, Catherine simply did not figure. She was the model to the missionaries of the Indian whose penances had no touch of egotism, and who was therefore docile. She showed the unmistakable sign in them of being a Christian; for she was both fierce and tender, fierce in her zeal, yet ready always to be a child in God's hands.

Catherine was unique at Caughnawaga, unique to her companions, not because of her dress, not because of her ingenuity in penances, but because of the flashes of Christian graces in her. She was wise. She could give good counsel. She had the gift of joy. And what patience was hers!

But beginning with good counsel, there are various stories of the good advice she gave. What is most evident in them is that with all her zeal she was fully conscious of the frailty of human nature. She did not try to turn others into other editions of herself. Perhaps the best story to illustrate this is a story of Catherine after she had gone to heaven. Two Iroquois maidens prayed to her, for her intercession. Would she not see to it that they could live a life dedicated to God as virgins, as she had led it? But if that was against God's will they preferred not to live at all. According to the story, which has its hush and its grandeur, within six months both the maidens were dead.

We can guess that many enthusiasts came to Catherine before her death with similar resolutions, and though no doubt she encouraged many to what was heroic, numerically she did more dissuading than exhorting. Like Madame Acarie, she had a discernment of souls. She knew when to encourage, when to discourage. One day a young married couple came to her. The husband's name was Francis Tsonnatonan, or in English, Francis Big-Mouth. He was only twenty-one, and his wife Marguerite was even younger. Both of them wished in some extraordinary way to show their love for God. Francis Big-Mouth asked for Catherine's advice. They were thinking, though married, of continuing to live together only as brother and sister.

The years to come were to bring Francis many tribulations. He was to be crippled and to live for fourteen years bent double, gaining his livelihood carving pipes and repairing kettles, and as he bent-double over his work, there would be dangling round his neck a relic of the Catherine he had once asked for advice. Terrible would be his sufferings and his humiliations, and terrible would be the hardships of his wife caring for his sufferings. I wonder if Catherine foresaw this future as she looked at the young couple, and studied them so tenderly, so penetratingly, so directly. At any rate she passed judgment on their resolve with a sagacity which could not have been wiser, had she been able to see into the future.

She began by asking Francis to say what he had to say. Then she turned to Marguerite. Both of them were equally zealous in their resolve. Yet Catherine did not congratulate them, nor encourage them. She decided that they must be made to drop their undertaking, but must be so made to do without hurting their feelings. Therefore she sent them to Father Frémin. She knew what his decision would be. Thus she showed a firmness in coming to her decision, as well as a gentleness in breaking it to them.

Catherine was looked up to for her wisdom, and sought after for the charm of her cheerfulness. Both her biographer priests used a word describing her, which though it was used frequently in the devotional writings of the early seventeenth century does not find a place often in the Jesuit Relations, not in describing the Indians : gaité, gaiety. Catherine according to Father Cholenec had "a surprising gaiety." "She was always gay," he says, "always content." Never was there any sign of chagrin in her at any disappointment. So marked was her gaiety that it was ever contagious, and it was left to the Sault by Catherine as a heritage. At her burial there was no mourning; there was public rejoicing.*

It would be futile to go on trying to make a list of the qualities which the Indians admired in Catherine, and for which they made her their spiritual leader; it would also be inappropriate, for the Indians did not analyse, nor love her for this or that. They loved her because she was Catherine, and Catherine was, as a holy Christian, what all holy Christians are and have been, a paradox. She was both fierce and gentle, humble and mastering, zealous and patient, sorrowful and cheerful, warlike and peace-ful, relentless, all-forgiving. It was as a paradox she was loved and found unique, for all her friends knew Indians who were fierce, and courageous, and others who were mild and forgiving, and they may even have known an Indian who was mild one day and ferocious the next according as his pulsebeat changed, but contradictions were fused in Catherine. She was two things at the same time. She had that mark of saintliness.

The paradox in any saintly person has always a glorious importance as an evidence of something unearthly. In Catherine's case the paradox that she was, had a peculiar significance, and timeliness. Through her mother she was descended from the passive long-suffering Algonquians; through her father from the active, aggressive Iroquoians. From one blood she inherited the Algonquian resignation to God's will, from the other the will of men to help themselves. Catherine

* Cholenec, p. 64.

as a Christian could be both Iroquois and Algonquin. She could accept absolutely God's omnipotence, and humble herself into a joyous obedience to doing things as He wished to have them done. At the same time she could become a part of the Mystical Body of Christ. Christ, too, had His long-house, for His Iroquois. In that new long-house she could dare all for Christ, suffer all for Him, be all by Him. She lost none of the cruelty of the Iroquois, but her cruelty was to herself, against pride, against self-complacence, against self-deception. Her Iroquois fore-fathers had bred her for the Church Militant, violent to be triumphant.

Catherine, after her persecutions were over, became loved at Caughnawaga. She became "The Christian" there, as before she had become so suddenly "The Christian" at Kana-waké. This speaks well for the progress Catherine had been able to make in a year at the Mission, and well too for the progress she had been able to make in her whole young life of twenty-two years. But also it speaks well for the discernment of the Indians who saw her daily, yet perceived her extraordinary quality, who were not blinded by envy, nor distracted from what was essential in her to some trivial detail. A remark by Father Cholenec gives us a very pretty and very profound picture of Catherine and Catherine's part at the Sault : all the other Indians liked to be near her in the chapel, so that they could pray better.

CHAPTER XI

TEKAKWITHA'S DEATH

CATHERINE had passed her first winter at the mission, not at Caughnawaga but in the woods, and in the woods she had given an example of how an Indian woman could live while on the hunt. She had passed the second winter in the settlement itself, showing there how an Indian woman, vowed to perpetual virginity, could live. The third winter she showed the Indians how an Indian Christian woman could die.

Catherine had been very near death in her first childhood, for she had lain sick of the small-pox in the same bed with her father, mother and brother, all of whom died of the disease, and all of whom had reached out their hands to drag her with them. She undoubtedly had after-effects of that sickness, aside from her pock-marks. Her eyes, as I have already mentioned, may have been weakened, and, as I have not mentioned, her health may have been given a turn which caused the head-aches which her director discovered had perpetually assaulted her, though without ever making her testy. But in spite of the after-effects she grew to be a very vigorous Indian maiden, one to whom it was nothing to trek three hundred miles from the Mohawk River to Caughnawaga ; one to whom it was no particular effort to do a lumberman's labor of felling trees, toppling over such large ones with a dull hatchet, that once she was almost killed by their top-pling ; one to whom the hardships of the hunt seemed luxu-ries. Catherine, it seemed, had left death behind her, death, at least, due to any bodily frailty.

And yet before her twenty-third year was well on, it was evident that she was direfully sick. What her malady was can be guessed at by the physicians who care to read what Fathers Cholenec and Chauchetière wrote about it.

Her head-aches came to be accompanied by vomitings, and then by the sweat of a slow-fever. Her last four months in this world were spent largely in bed — or rather on her fur mat — on one of those curious sleeping shelves in her Iroquois long-house. How she came to have to retire to bed we can-not well say. There were some at the Sault who shook their heads and said that she had practiced too great austerities. Notably her indiscretion in spending three nights sleeping on thorns was blamed to having her look pale as a corpse. Others attributed her unhappy weakening to a walk she had taken over the ice to La Prairie, with Marie Thérèse. She had grown overheated by carrying a heavy burden on her way back, and a cold had set in. It is more likely, however, that neither her penances nor her overheating had much to do with her decline. It is likely her malady was but taking its course. Austerities have been known to prolong life rather than to shorten it. A winter walk for Catherine when she was well was nothing, or might have killed her then and there. As it was, Catherine's decline was gradual. She did not die until four months after the walk. Yet soon after the walk she did retire to bed.

One thing is sure : she must have been very feeble or she would have risen from bed, for she did not like to surrender, nor to notice her ailments. She never complained of headaches or showed that she had them. She never said in regard to her sufferings : "Enough." She asked for more. Unless forbidden so to do, she would have added voluntary penances and fastings to the penances and fastings which God's Will had given her. Her greatest pleasure, even when she was permanently in bed, was to drag herself to the church to the presence of the Blessed Sacrament, there to pray. It was not easy : she had to cling to a bench to keep herself from falling to the ground. Yet there were days and days when she could not go to the chapel, not even crawling on hands and knees. Week after week she had to acknowledge herself helpless. She lay as motionless as a beaver-pelt on the shelf of her longhouse, yet with her heart awake, her heart at prayer.

It was no happy state for anyone to be sick at the Christian Sault in dead of winter. The village was short-handed. All save the aged and the children had gone forth to the hunt. Most of the members of the Holy Family Confraternity had gone. There was no one to nurse the sick, and Catherine was sick. The elderly left behind had their own work to do. The only work they could do for Catherine was to leave a bowl of sagamité and a cup of water near the shelf on which she suffered. She did not even have the privilege of being treated as one who is surely taking the great step : death. She lived on, week after week, not in delirium, not facing a crisis, but simply an inconvenient invalid, humbled as her energy hated to be humbled.

It was during this time that Catherine became very grateful to Father Chauchetière. He, of a modest retiring disposition, and of great delicacy, had hitherto had little directly to do with Catherine, for Father Cholenec, his superior, was very naturally her director. But now in default of the members of the Holy Family Confraternity, he took to visiting Catherine. Her one pleasure was to hear about God, particularly about the life of Our Lord. Father Chauchetière,* more poetical than philosophical, was excellently suited to describe the great events of Christ's life vividly to her. And also he had albums of pictures which represented figuratively the mysteries of the Faith. It was a delight to him to explain these, but his greater delight was to see her delight in hearing what he explained. Her body was in Purgatory. Her mind, at these tales of God's goodness, was in Heaven.

So edified was he by the seraphic joy of this wasting corpse that he wished others to be edified. Since most of the elderly were busy, he called the children, who were busy only at play, to her bed-side. Catherine, who was known for her silence, became talkative to the children in explaining to them in her own Iroquois words Father Chauchetière's pretty pictures.

These visits to Catherine meant much to the children at the Sault. A whole generation grew up remembering her voice. The visits meant also much to Father Chauchetière. His conviction of her sanctity, which he feared nobody else could understand, came to him in these days. But also they

---

* In Chauchetière's Life of Tekakwitha, written in 1695 and still preserved in MS. in the Collège de Ste.-Marie at Montreal, the style and the hand-writing give us an idea of its author's character.

meant more to Catherine, and it is a very tender story that
Father Cholenec — not mentioning Father Chauchetière's
name — tells of how Catherine was so grateful to Father
Chauchetière, that she appeared to him several times in visions
after her death, and gave him various messages. It seems that
Father Chauchetière, whose life had never experienced any
extraordinary trances — like those of Madame Acarie, or
Marie de L'Incarnation, for instance — was ravished into several five-hour trances by the visitor, whom he had visited
while she was on earth. So proud was he of these visits and
touched by them that in his life of Catherine he did not mention them as having occurred to him himself. They had
happened to a certain priest. That priest, he said, had been
told many things which afterwards came true. Also the priest
had been commanded by Catherine to draw her picture.
Since he could not draw, and merely liked looking at pictures, he at first hesitated. Then he had complied, after he
had been commanded. Hence we have the picture of his
picture in the frontispiece of this book.

As the winter drew on and on, more and more people came
to visit Catherine, not so much to give help as to receive counsel. Catherine had now a special right to speak. She was
singing her Iroquois death-song. Dying Iroquois had a traditional prestige. They were listened to, and therefore the
missionaries had availed themselves of the prestige by using
the dying Christians as their most persuasive preachers. Many
conversions had thus been made by the dying. And now that
it became evident that Catherine was dying, she had a special
way of being persuasive, so joyous she was, so evidently a

happy Christian. Catherine was preaching from the cross. The missionaries encouraged the tepid, the uncertain, the pagans even, to visit her, and to hear what the next world said. And as she was speaking the hunting parties began to trail back to the Sault.

Finally on Tuesday in Holy Week came the Visitor of Visitors. It was the custom of Caughnawaga that the Holy Eucharist was never brought to the Indians in their houses, for the houses had not the privacy of a European cottage. They were the gathering places of a clan. The dying or sick Indian who was to receive Holy Communion for his restoration to health or happy death, was carried on a litter of birch-bark to the chapel itself, and there he received the Holy Viaticum. But Catherine was too weak to be moved. And, besides, she was exceptional. She had sanctified the roof under which she asked God to stoop. On Tuesday of Holy Week, April 16th, 1680, God, as I say, came to her. Christ came in His Flesh and Blood to visit one who had made herself another Christ to welcome Him. She received Him also in her best outward Mohawk comeliness by borrowing a tunic from Marie Thérèse, her own clothing having turned to tatters.

After having received Our Lord, Catherine appeared to be weakening, and the priests decided that her hour was near ; they prepared to anoint her. She assured them, however, that there was no hurry. They could wait till the next day. It seemed as if she lived no longer in the world, our world, and could know things that we do not know.

For instance, on Tuesday night she saw things we cannot

see. By this time, although some of the Indians were still off on their hunt, most of the bands had returned, and the Confraternity of the Holy Family was at its work. Two members of it were watching Catherine day and night. During the night one of the watchers was a young girl who wished to do something special for Catherine, and going out into the woods she whipped herself till the blood flowed. Then she came back, and when they were alone, Catherine spoke to her, telling her of what she had done. The watcher protested, but Catherine calmly told her she had seen her doing this penance for her sake. She would remember her — she said — in Heaven.

Catherine, as an unbaptized Iroquois girl, had never indulged in dreams. She had an aversion to them, and she still had. Her characteristic was a sober sense, a complete lack of flightiness, or whimsical self-delusion. She was trusted by her directors not for anything spectacular but for her constancy, what Father Chauchetière calls her "esprit solide." Even as she drew near death she had no trances. Yet she did now and then reveal strange knowledges. Sometime before her last sickness she had been talking with her friends at the cemetery. "Where shall we be buried?" "There is where I shall lie," said Catherine. After she was dead Father Chauchetière, who knew nothing of the saying, wished that she might be buried in the chapel. Father Cholenec, who likewise knew nothing of the saying, wished her to be buried in the place which she happened to have indicated. Since Father Cholenec was commander, what she had prophesied was done by Him. This incident may prove no more than that a coincidence happened, yet it is coincidence that touches the heart.

The day-light of Wednesday in Holy Week arrived. Catherine received Extreme Unction. There were many people round her praying. One of them, of course, was her companion, Marie Thérèse. This woman, inseparable from Catherine, Catherine sent away from her. She knew that Marie Thérèse had work to do in the forest bringing in wood. Let her go out to her work. She would call Marie Thérèse if death approached. And how could she know when death would approach ?

Marie Thérèse went out to her work, and sure enough, she did receive a summons from Catherine. What Catherine then said to her, Father Chauchetière, also present, could not help hearing.

"I am leaving you," said Catherine. "I am going to die. Remember always what we have done together since first we met. If you change I shall accuse you before the tribunal of God. Take courage, despise the discoursings of those who have not the Faith. If they ever try to persuade you to marry, listen only to the Fathers. If you cannot serve God here, go to the Mission at Lorette. Don't give up your mortifications. I shall love you in Heaven. I shall pray for you. I shall aid you."

This was an Iroquois who was speaking, unmistakably an Iroquois. So strong yet so tender. A Christian Iroquois to another Iroquois : "I shall aid you."

After that, she kept an Algonquian silence, or the silence of any man-born child who is dying. Father Chauchetière watched her. She seemed more to be contemplating than suffering. There was no struggle. He did notice a twinge in the neck. It was three o'clock in the afternoon. She was dead.

It was three o'clock in the afternoon that she died, and there were still some hours left before the April darkness would come to dim the dim long-house, but before the darkness came a transformation took place in Catherine's visage. A kind of glorification of this Indian girl was enacted before the Indians. It seemed not only as if her hood had at last been thrown back — as it was — but as if she had torn a pock-marked mask from her face. The pock-marks were still there. Yet she shone. They had never seen her before. Thereupon the Indians behaved as they had never before behaved with one of their dead. The women did not wail. The men did not crouch about her, stoic. They pressed near to her with delight. They went farther, thought Father Chauchetière, than they should have done. They behaved like many simple, direct, peoples in the Middle Ages, of whom they had never heard, and had not the slightest desire to imitate. They kissed the hands of the empty body. They tore from its dress tatters that they could preserve as keepsakes. They did, if you wish, exactly the opposite from what their ancestors had done to their dead in the days of pagan waiting. The ancestors had given to the dead the best they had. Now they took from the dead their riches of riches. It was they who were in need. She it was who was happy. Now they were remembering the dead but in a new way.

The next day, Holy Thursday, Caughnawaga buried Catherine's body. It was a day singularly fitted for her burial, for she had had an heroic devotion for the Holy Eucharist which had been instituted on that day. And all that was connected with her burial was also fitting. At Catherine Gandeakena's funeral there had been no throwing of gifts into the grave. At Catherine Tekakwitha's there was not even sorrow. There was nothing but joy. It was not merely that a human soul, whom they happened to know and to consider holy, had gone to Paradise, there to remember them, there to plead for them. It was that one of their flesh and blood and with their ways had very visibly gone to the Christian Paradise and made it their Paradise. They could see into it more easily now. They could even take a pride in it, for from it looked down on them one who was so clearly a Christian — Catherine — and so unmistakably an Indian — Tekakwitha.

BIBLIOGRAPHY

The following works have been cited in the foregoing pages :

Beauchamp, W. W., *A History of the New York Iroquois.* New York, 1905.

Bremond, H., *Histoire Littéraire du Sentiment Religieux en France,* Vol. II. Paris, 1930.

Brinton, D. H. *The Lenapé and their Legends.* Philadelphia, 1885.

Burrage, H. S., (ed.), *Early English and French Voyages.* New York, 1930.

Buteux, J., *Narré de la Prise du Père Isaac Jogues* (tr. in The Pilgrim of Our Lady of Martyrs), January-December, 1896.

Cartier, Jacques, *The Voyages of Jacques Cartier,* ed. H. P. Biggar. Ottawa, 1924.

Champlain, Samuel de, *Voyages.* New York, 1907.

Chauchetière, Claude, *Vie de la Bonne Catherine Tegahkouita.* (Of this the ms. written in 1695 is preserved at Collège Sainte-Marie, Montreal. It was once printed by J. Munsell, 1887).

Cholenec, Pierre, *Vie de Catherine Tegakouita, Premiére Viérge Irokoise.* (This life written in 1717 and preserved in ms. at the Collège Sainte-Marie, Montreal ; has never been printed).

Cooper, J. M., *The Northern Algonquin Supreme Being* (Catholic University of America, Anthropological Series No. 2). Washington, 1934.

Dorsey, G. A., *The Arapaho Sun Dance, the Ceremony of the Offering Lodge* (Field Columbian Museum Publ., Anthrop. Series), Vol. IV. Chicago, 1903.

Harrington, M. R., *Religion and Ceremonies of the Lenapé* (Heye Foundation monographs). New York, 1921.

Hale, H. (ed.), *The Iroquois Book of Rites.* Philadelphia, 1883.

Innes, H. A., *The Fur Trade in Canada.* New Haven, 1930.

Lafitau, J. F., *Moeurs des Sauvages Américains*. Paris, 1724.

Marie de L'Incarnation, *Ecrits Spirituels,* Ed Jamet. Paris, 1929.

Morgan, L. H., *League of the Ho-De'-Ho-San-Nee or Iroquois* (This was originally published in 1851, but the edition here referred to is that annotated by H. M. Lloyd, 2 vols.) New York, 1901.

Parker, A. C., *History of the State of New York,* Chapter "Iroquois," in Vol. I. New York, 1933.

Parkman, F., *The Jesuits in North America.* Boston, 1909.

Prescott, W. H., *Conquest of Mexico.* Philadelphia, 1869.

Radin, P., *The Story of the American Indian.* New York, 1934.

Radisson, P. E., *Voyages,* Publications of Prince Society. Boston, 1885. (This relation by a "coureur du bois" who sought for English patronage was written by him in very pithy, colloquial, yet definitely broken English.)

Rochemonteix, C. de, S.J., *Les Jésuites et la Nouvelle France au XVII Siècle* (3 vols.). Paris, 1896.

Sagard-Théodat, F. G., *Le Grand Voyage au Pays des Hurons.* Paris, 1632.

Salone, E., *La Colonisation de la Nouvelle France.* Paris.

Schmidt, W. (1) *Die Ursprung der Gottesidee,* 5 vols. Munster, 1911.
        (2) *The Origin and Growth of Religion* (tr. H. J. Rose). New York, 1931.
        (3) *The High Gods of North America.* Oxford, 1933.

Smith, Captain, John, *Travels and Works,* ed. Sir George Percy. New York, 1910.

Talbot, F. X., S.J., *Saint among Savages.* New York, 1935.

Thwaites, R. G., ed., *Jesuit Relations and Allied Documents,* 73 vols. Cleveland, 1896-1901.

Williams, Roger, *Key into the Language of America* (Collection of the Rhode Island Historical Society, Vol. I), 1827.

Willoughby, C. C., *Antiquities of New England Indians.* Cambridge, (Mass.), 1935.